The Archaeology of
Medieval London

The Archaeology of Medieval London

CHRISTOPHER THOMAS

SUTTON PUBLISHING

First published in 2002 by
Sutton Publishing Limited · Phoenix Mill
Thrupp · Stroud · Gloucestershire · GL5 2 BU

British Library Cataloguing in Publication Data
A catalogue record for this book is available from the British Library.

ISBN 0 7509 2718 6

Typeset in 11.5/15 pt Garamond.
Typesetting and origination by
Sutton Publishing Limited.
Printed and bound in England by
J.H. Haynes & Co. Ltd, Sparkford.

Contents

List of Figures

Acknowledgements

This book combines the work of many archaeologists over a long period of time, particularly my colleagues at the Museum of London Archaeology Service. It was the idea of Dr John Schofield, to whom I am grateful for advice. I am particularly indebted to those who have allowed me access to works which remain as yet unpublished: in particular Barney Sloane for St Mary Clerkenwell, Barney Sloane and Gordon Malcolm for St John's Clerkenwell, Alison Steele for Bermondsey Priory, Julian Ayre, Robin Wroe-Brown and Dick Malt for Thames Court, John Schofield for Holy Trinity Priory, Ian Grainger for St Mary Graces and Derek Seeley for Winchester Palace. I am also indebted to them for the use of illustrations, vital to this book, but also, as yet, unpublished. Fig. 6 was drawn by Damian Goodburn, Figs 10 and 29 by Judith Dobie, Fig. 13 by Peter Jackson and Figs 45 and 46 by Mark Samuel.

The drawings were produced by Tracy Wellman and Helen Jones and the photographs by Andy Chopping, Maggie Cox and the author. The maps of London for each period are based upon those produced in *The archaeology of Greater London: an assessment of archaeological evidence for human presence in the area now covered by Greater London* (MoLAS 2000) and *Aspects of Saxo-Norman London: 1 Building and street development* (Horsman, Milne and Milne 1988). I would like to thank Taryn Nixon for supporting this book and for allowing me access to Museum of London Archaeology Service resources and material.

I am also indebted to Monica Kendall who edited the text and to my colleagues for their comments and suggestions, in particular John Schofield, Liz Barham and Barney Sloane. Their ideas and contributions have been of enormous value but, as usual, any errors remain the responsibility of the author.

Introduction

The title of this book contains three words all of which need definition. The word 'medieval' describes a period over which much debate has raged concerning the date of both its beginning and its end. The most common dates used are 1066 to 1485. This book takes a slightly wider viewpoint and the thinking behind this is described in both the first chapter and the last section of chapter 4. In summary, it takes the reoccupation of the walled city of London in the late ninth century as its starting point and concludes at the Dissolution of the Monasteries in the 1540s. Secondly, while this book is intended to be an 'archaeological' description it is by no means confined only to that. To try to describe and discuss a picture of medieval life without using documentary, pictorial or cartographic evidence would be to put only part of the story across, so where those aspects of London's history are relevant they have been included. Thirdly, Greater London now covers an enormous area of some 670 square miles but this includes many small settlements and villages that were not part of London until its huge expansion in the seventeenth, eighteenth, nineteenth and twentieth centuries. For that reason I am covering here the historic core of London: the medieval city with its immediate hinterland, the main suburb across London Bridge in Southwark and the royal and ecclesiastical centre at Westminster. Finally, it would be impossible for any book to cover all that is known about the archaeology of medieval London as there is so much information. This book, therefore, aims to summarise it and to put it into perspective. The bibliography is not comprehensive and not every statement has been given a reference. It lists a large number of volumes, some general, and many more that are site specific produced by my MoLAS colleagues. The reader is directed towards these for more detailed information.

London's dominance of the United Kingdom is clear to all today whether or not they agree with it, but what was its position during the medieval period? Its influence in terms of both trade and politics is discussed in this book and while it may not have been as large as some of its counterparts in Europe, such as Paris, it dominated England in a way that other capitals did not. It was by a long way the largest city in the kingdom, with a population perhaps four times that of its nearest rivals; that London dominated the entire region is beyond question but its effect upon its immediate surroundings was even more profound.

Archaeology has had a chequered history in London. Some records of standing structures were made in the eighteenth, nineteenth and early twentieth centuries, and then occasional periods of good-quality work were carried out, such as that by Professor Grimes in the 1940s and 1950s. But sustained high-quality archaeological recording did not begin until the mid-1970s. Much of our knowledge, therefore, is based upon investigations carried out after that date, although work from earlier archaeologists and antiquarians is included in this book and forms an important area of knowledge, particularly for such sites as the Palace of Westminster.

Much of the medieval city of London was destroyed in the Great Fire of 1666 and there was further destruction during the Blitz and through the development of London in the Victorian period and the twentieth century, often with little or no archaeological record. The same development led to much destruction of medieval London in the areas outside the city which were unaffected by the Great Fire. Other historical events such as the Dissolution of the Monasteries also had a profound effect upon London's surviving medieval buildings. In many cases it is even difficult to see the ancient street pattern. There are, however, still a handful of surviving medieval structures including parts of the Palace and Abbey at Westminster, part of the Bishop of Winchester's palace in Southwark, the Tower of London and a section of the city wall, and parts of the monasteries of St Mary Overie (now Southwark Cathedral), St Bartholomew's and St John's Priory Clerkenwell. Because of the huge loss of the standing structures of medieval London, the remains beneath the ground are of even greater importance. Archaeology can tell us so much about the buildings, layout and development of medieval London and about the lifestyle, diet and health of medieval Londoners.

It is this information which should concern us most. How did London develop and why did it become such a dominant factor in the life, trade, religion and economy of England? How was it able to sustain itself and its population? How did those people live? What did they eat? What did their buildings look like? How did they compare over time and with other parts of the country? How did the average person's lifestyle differ from that of the wealthiest? What was the attitude of Londoners to the Church and religion?

These are just some of the questions posed in this book. We do not know all the answers but we can go some way to painting a true picture of life in London during the medieval period.

CHAPTER 1

London before the Norman Conquest

INTRODUCTION

The starting point chosen here for the beginnings of medieval London is the reoccupation of the city in 886 and the formation of London as a 'burgh': a defended settlement. Prior to that point, Londoners had abandoned the old Roman walled city in favour of a new settlement along the Strand, known as Lundenwic, which grew up in the seventh century and became a major mercantile centre.

Lundenwic is one of the great success stories of modern archaeology in London. The site of the Middle Saxon settlement was discovered only in 1985 and its scope is now much better understood. It covered the area roughly from Kingsway in the east to Trafalgar Square in the west, and from the Thames in the south – at that time some distance back from the modern riverfront – to Oxford Street in the north. Initially the settlement may have been small, based around the riverfront and the Strand. Soon the settlement expanded to take in an area of about 60 hectares (almost 150 acres). The major excavations at the Royal Opera House have now given us a better picture of the town which was described in the eighth century by Bede as a trading centre. At the Royal Opera House site a road was found leading down to the Thames, flanked by drains and with narrow alleys leading off it. Between the alleys lay houses made of timber and wattle and daub. Environmental and finds evidence shows that many industries were practised here, including weaving, metalworking and boneworking. The settlement thrived and prospered until the Viking attacks of the mid-ninth century.

Across the River Fleet to the east, a few Middle Saxon artefacts have been recovered from the area of the old walled Roman city. Documentary evidence tells us that Mellitus was installed as Bishop of London in 604, suggesting that St Paul's was founded at that time – and indeed these artefacts have mostly been found in the western side of the city. It has been suggested that there was a royal establishment in the north-west corner of the city, within the old Roman fort (the name 'Aldermanbury' refers to the enclosure of the Ealdorman, a Late Saxon term) but there is as yet no archaeological evidence for a palace here.

Viking raids in the 840s and 850s – with London, Canterbury and Rochester all stormed – must have had a serious effect upon both trading and the morale of the population. Evidence from the Royal Opera House excavations suggests that Lundenwic may already have been shrinking by the middle of the ninth century, a process no doubt made worse by the Viking attacks. From 874 London appears to have been under Viking control and it may be that the Vikings had attacked the walled city and captured it in 872. Presumably to give themselves greater means of defence, Londoners reoccupied the old Roman city and repaired its now decayed walls under the leadership of King Alfred.

The topographic position of the city cannot be fully understood by looking at it today, as significant changes have taken place. Along the western side of the city lay the River Fleet, where modern-day Farringdon Street now lies (the river is now carried beneath the street in a large culvert). The Fleet was wide and deep enough to be navigable in its lower reaches during the later Saxon and medieval periods. The land rises steeply from there up Ludgate Hill to the site of St Paul's Cathedral. The natural topography then gently drops away to the east. At the eastern end of Poultry, where the Bank of England and the Mansion House now stand, lay the River Walbrook. This was somewhat smaller than the Fleet and had been canalised during the Roman period. It flowed down from just to the west of where Liverpool Street station now stands, through the city, and entered the Thames south of the street which bears its name, Walbrook. The eastern side of the city was much flatter and continued up to the old Roman town walls which at this time ran through where the Tower of London now stands.

The history of the River Thames is crucially important to the understanding of the development of London. Rising sea levels since the melting of the ice caps from about 10000 BC have meant that the tidal head has moved further and further upriver, allowing boats greater and easier access to the higher reaches of London, brought in by the high tide. The story is not quite so simple, however, as river levels have also fallen at times over the last 10,000 years. The current understanding is that the tidal head had reached upstream of Westminster by 1200 BC, but falling river levels – a regression (owing to a fall in sea level) – had caused the tidal head to move back down to the city by the early Roman period, and beyond by the later Roman period. By the Saxon period rising river levels – a transgression – presumably allowed the trading emporium of Lundenwic to prosper, but a slight alteration in the tidal head of the river could have had a dramatic effect upon the ability of boats to access the ports and might even have affected the ability to trade. A sustained rise in the level of the river, no doubt aided by the progressive embanking and narrowing of the Thames, has led to a mostly continual rise in the river level over the last 800 years.

Archaeological evidence from Southwark and Westminster suggests widespread flooding of the environs of London in the early eleventh century, which is backed up by the description in the *Anglo-Saxon Chronicle* of a great flood on 28 September 1014, which came further inland than any previous flood had done (Watson *et al* 2001). In Southwark, archaeologists have found that large amounts of earlier deposits were scoured away and replaced by new river-laid deposits upstream of the bridge. That there were major floods even further upstream at this time can be seen at Westminster where much of the foreshore was washed away and new river-laid silts deposited on the higher reaches of the island in the early to mid-eleventh century (Thomas *et al* in prep).

LAYOUT AND DEVELOPMENT

When Alfred reoccupied London it was a fairly desolate place covered in trees, weeds and scrub, and surrounded by decayed Roman walls and gates. There was presumably a cathedral and attendant buildings at St Paul's, perhaps within its own precinct boundary, and there may also have been a royal enclosure, although no traces have been found. Alfred laid out a network of streets with little reference to the Roman road network, except for the entrances through the city walls (Fig. 1). Cheapside became the main east–west thoroughfare. Other streets ran south from this to the river, with the focus of the early settlement based around Aethelred's Hythe (later known as Queenhithe). The western street of this grid was formed by Bread Street, the eastern by Kennet Wharf Lane. There is also evidence of a second area of settlement of late ninth- or early tenth-century date to the east of the River Walbrook from around Fish Street Hill, which suggests that the settlement was bifocal with the twin areas of habitation occupying the higher ground on either side of the Walbrook Valley. The waterfront on the western side of the two areas seems to have been developed first.

During the later tenth century this grid of streets was expanded north of Cheapside, creating Milk Street and Ironmonger Lane. In the eleventh century Lawrence Lane was laid out north of Gresham Street. Houses and a church were built on either side of this narrow cobbled street, and archaeologists have found that the street extended beyond these buildings to the north, perhaps leading to a

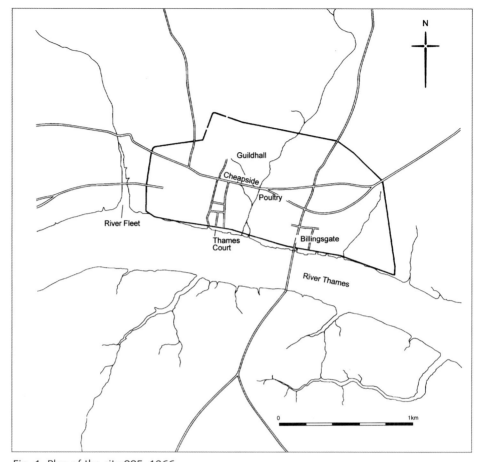

Fig. 1. Plan of the city 885–1066

predecessor of the later medieval Guildhall. The streets to the east and west of the lane curved around, still reflecting the shape of the ancient Roman amphitheatre.

HOUSES

Evidence for the early occupation of the western side of the city behind the riverfront has been recovered at the junction of Bow Lane, Watling Street and Basing Lane (now Cannon Street). Bow Lane appears to have been one of the early streets laid out in the post-Alfredian period in the city. Here, a line of pits about 12m behind the Bow Lane street frontage suggests that there had once been houses fronting on to the street, destroyed by later buildings. The pits were perhaps used for the disposal of rubbish in their back yards. One sunken-floored building, probably dating to between 850 and 1020, along the Bow

Lane frontage measured at least 4.5m by 4.9m and had a beaten earth floor (Schofield *et al* 1990, 46).

Similar sunken-floored structures were built a few metres to the north, on the eastern side of Bow Lane and north of Watling Street. The earliest building predated the original street surfaces of Bow Lane and so may be a very early building of this period, perhaps dating to the late ninth century. Further north was a second building, this time a surface-laid structure which was laid up against the gravel road of Bow Lane (Schofield *et al* 1990, 78).

In the first half of the eleventh century this building fronting the street was replaced by another timber structure with wattle-and-daub walls. It included a bread oven in its south-west corner. To the south lay a sunken-floored building which had posts in the corners but appeared to have been open sided. Within it were layers of carbonised grain which spread out over the edges of the building, suggesting it was related to the building containing the bread oven. A third building, also sunken-floored, lay some 11m behind the street frontage. It had timber walls and a porch that gave access from the east, which might suggest that it was accessed from a lane other than Bow Lane (Schofield *et al* 1990, 79).

Evidence for the development of the central area of the city has been greatly enhanced by the excavations at 1 Poultry during the 1990s. Along the Cheapside/

Fig. 2. A late Saxon building at No. 1 Poultry (photo: Museum of London Archaeology Service)

Poultry frontage sunken-floored buildings forming small dwellings were built in the late ninth century (Fig. 2). These buildings were all constructed of timber with posts and planks and sometimes wattle hurdles. They were subdivided into rooms and were floored in brickearth (the natural subsoil) or brushwood. The houses had yards which yielded large quantities of pig bone, suggesting that the occupants were rearing pigs. South of the houses lay a market. In the late tenth century the houses were replaced by a terrace of timber buildings, possibly shops (Rowsome 2000, 49–52).

The area to the west of the 1 Poultry site, at the junction of Cheapside and Queen Street, was on the edge of the original Alfredian resettlement of London and was not used for occupation until the tenth century. Large numbers of rubbish and/or cesspits indicate that Late Saxon Londoners lived nearby and were disposing of their refuse in an uninhabited area. The old east–west Roman road through the city was still exposed but the alignment of the pits suggests that it was no longer in use as a principal highway. The pits were all aligned with the medieval streets such as Cheapside and not with the old Roman roads (Hill and Woodger 1999, 24–5).

The earliest building activity here dated to the tenth century. There were two surface-laid buildings, one of which had a brickearth slab floor overlaid by occupation deposits and hearths. The two buildings varied widely in size, one being about 11m long and the other only 4m long. Dendrochronological dating of this latter building indicates that it was probably built in 913 and went out of use only five years later. There were also sunken-floored buildings here, two of which were aligned along either side of the old Roman road, suggesting that it was still in evidence and might even have been in use as a back alley. The southern building was probably a domestic dwelling built in the second or third quarters of the tenth century. The walls consisted of horizontally laid planks held in place by posts, and the floor was of beaten earth. After the building had gone out of use it was used as a midden. The northern building was aligned end on to the former Roman road and was sunk 0.5m below it. It measured about 2m by 5–6m. The east and west walls were constructed in the same way as the earlier building but the southern wall differed in having a ground beam which presumably reflects the site of the entrance into the building from the old road surface. The lack of an obvious floor surface and its relatively small size suggest it was not a dwelling but more likely a workshop. It contained iron slag in its earliest phase but not in a later phase when it was more likely to have been an outbuilding. This slag contained parts of hearth linings, hearth bottoms and hammerscale, all typical of the debris from a smithy, no doubt located nearby.

Late tenth- or early eleventh-century sunken-floored buildings have also been found in the southern part of the city: about 200m south-east of St Paul's to the south of Cannon Street, at Bucklersbury and further north at Wood Street (Grimes 1968, 156–9).

Houses to the north of Cheapside seem to be somewhat later, perhaps late tenth century in date, reflecting the later expansion into this area (Schofield *et al* 1990, 113–17, 151–2). At Milk Street in 1976 the ubiquitous 'dark earth' – a layer of dark silt regularly found covering Roman deposits in the city and Southwark, and covering Middle Saxon deposits in Lundenwic – was found up to 1m thick. This layer is often thought to include the upper (and therefore latest) deposits from the relevant periods, later mixed by a variety of factors. One building found within the dark earth was a sunken-floored building, at least 1.5m deep, which fronted on to an old Roman road on the east side of the site, indicating that the road was still visible and in use at this time. To the east, the dark earth did not cover one Roman road, suggesting the road was still in use then, but late tenth-century buildings cut into the road, indicating its disuse. By the eleventh century a new building was constructed over the old Roman road, suggesting that it had completely gone out of use by this time. On the west side of the site there were two successive ground-level buildings constructed against the Milk Street frontage. No other structures were found along this frontage and the lack of pits in the areas behind may suggest again that development along Milk Street was only sporadic at this time. One eleventh-century pit contained crucible fragments and another contained pots with pigment stains, probably of madder, a purple dye (Schofield *et al* 1990, 117).

Some of the best evidence for the development of the northern part of the city has come from the excavations beneath Guildhall Yard (Bateman 2000, 46–57). Here a wealth of eleventh-century material was recovered, some of which definitely dates to the pre-Conquest period. One of the major finds on this site has been the discovery of the Roman amphitheatre. By the tenth century this had become a disused, uninhabited muddy hollow. During the eleventh century the ground level was raised to flatten out the ground between the old banks of the arena seating. On the north side, pits were dug to dispose of domestic refuse, presumably by the nearby inhabitants, wattle fences were erected as cattle corrals and ditches were dug to drain the ground.

One sunken-floored timber building predating the eleventh century was found to the east of Lawrence Lane, but the remainder all dated to the eleventh century. In general, the buildings on either side of Lawrence Lane were very different in character (Fig. 3). Those on the west were all wattle-built and were

N

Lawrence Lane

houses

churchyard and
burials

0   20m

Fig. 3. Plan of the house development along Lawrence Lane at the Guildhall

positioned end on to the lane; the environmental evidence suggests they were a mixture of low-status dwellings and stables and pens for animals. One was 10m long by 5m wide and entered by a doorway from the south. It was divided into three rooms and had beaten earth floors. The room leading off the entrance in the centre contained a bench on its south wall for sitting and perhaps sleeping. The eastern room had a hearth while the western room was the kitchen, also containing a hearth. Associated with these houses were numerous rubbish pits containing the discarded items of everyday life, including a wooden mallet. The buildings on the eastern side of the lane were built from posts and planks and were probably higher-status dwellings. The outside of the buildings was probably lined with turves, and the roofs in turf, thatch, boards or shingles. The largest building on this side of the lane was built around the middle of the eleventh century but clearly continued on into the twelfth. It measured about 9m by 5m and was divided into three rooms, the central one containing hearths. There was a distinctly Danish and Scandinavian influence in the area around the Guildhall in both the style of its buildings and the finds.

Behind the Queenhithe dock the earliest domestic buildings found probably date to the early eleventh century, although it remains possible that there were much earlier buildings there (Ayre *et al* in prep). Initially the Roman quayside wall was dismantled on either side of the inlet to allow access through it out on to the reclaimed land. The western side of Queenhithe remained undeveloped, in direct contrast to that to the east. The extraordinarily fragmentary nature of the buildings and the constant reuse and repair of walls make the number of buildings impossible to ascertain for certain, but the excavators have identified perhaps twelve buildings of this date. All of the structures were timber-built and laid at ground level, unlike the sunken-floored buildings often seen on drier land. These buildings were, by and large, wattle- or timber-built with either earth or plank floors which were covered in sedges or rushes and damp organic matter full of insects. The roofs were probably thatched; the large number of burnt posts suggests that many were destroyed or at least damaged by fire. One building had an internal dimension of 5.5m and a large central post suggesting a gable-end wall. The most completely excavated building had internal dimensions of 4m by 8m, later expanded to 6m by 11m. One large post-built structure was possibly an aisled building. The surviving posts were of the same diameter as the remarkable reused aisle posts found in the revetments (see below), although those posts were clearly earlier. An unusual survival was a building containing an oven, almost 1m in diameter, with wattle-supported brickearth walls containing a considerable amount of carbonised grain (Ayre *et al* in prep).

DAILY LIFE

The inhabitants of Late Saxon London probably produced a sizeable amount of their own food and other necessities and traded through bartering more often than cash. Most buildings were of timber and simply built, but finds from around the Queenhithe dock suggest some goods were imported.

The large amounts of animal bones found in the rubbish pits associated with the buildings around the Queenhithe dock indicate part of the diet of the inhabitants of London and that they were breeding animals such as sheep or goats. They also ate eggs – shown by the number of female chicken and goose bones found. The animals kept by these Londoners were of a variety of ages: sheep were kept for a while for wool before being slaughtered, and female cows were used for milk, while the pigs were all slaughtered young. Game such as deer, hare and duck suggests that Londoners hunted local wild animals. Marine fish such as eel and flatfish were probably caught in the estuary, and naturally freshwater fish like roach and bream, and spawning fish like salmon and trout, were also eaten (Ayre *et al* in prep). The ubiquitous molluscs – oyster, mussel and cockle – were found in large numbers and provided an important part of the Late Saxon diet, as they seem to have done in the Roman period and throughout the medieval period.

Some fragments of clothing from this time have survived. A lead-alloy disc brooch, pieces of woollen cloth and leather shoes were found along Cheapside (Hill and Woodger 1999, 29–41), similar material at Milk Street where a horn comb was also recovered (Schofield *et al* 1990, 113–15) and a selection of footwear survives from No. 1 Poultry (Fig. 4).

Fig. 4. Tenth-century leather boots and shoes from the site of No. 1 Poultry (photo: MoLAS)

MARKETS

Londoners bought some of their goods and produce in shops and markets. One such market was established in the late ninth century to the south of dwellings along Cheapside/Poultry and west of the River Walbrook. The market had gravel and cobble surfaces and seems also to have been used as a rubbish tip. By the late tenth century a terrace of timber buildings, possibly shops, had been built along both Poultry and Bucklersbury. It may be that the growth of London created the need for shops along the main roads to cater for the increase in trade. Trades practised here seem to have included iron- and boneworking. Bone artefacts found include handles, combs and gaming pieces (Rowsome 2000, 49–52).

Finds from the dockside areas suggest that some goods were imported – these include Northumbrian coins dating to 843–55, amulets, sixteen hooked tags (a form of dress fastening), brooches, a copper-alloy comb and lead mounts. These came from as far afield as Domburg (now in the Netherlands) and Scandinavia, and some from the Carolingian empire. Most seem to be of ninth-century date (Ayre *et al* in prep).

DOCKS AND LONDON BRIDGE

The old Roman riverside wall probably still existed for most if not all of its length by the time of the reoccupation of the city, while the river seems to have been eroding the old Roman timber revetments, still partially exposed on the gravel foreshore (Steedman *et al* 1992, 99). There is evidence that gates led through this wall on to the foreshore to the east of London Bridge and at Queenhithe.

Queenhithe

Excavations at Thames Court on the site of Queenhithe have produced some of the earliest and most important information for the early years of the reoccupation of the walled city (Ayre *et al* in prep). There was no archaeological evidence of structural activity before the creation of Alfred's port, and up to 1.5m of silt had accumulated over the old Roman quay, which indicated various changes in the river level and the flow of water.

The most surprising finds from the site were two burials laid on the foreshore. One was a female laid on her back with her head to the west. She had been laid on a bed of reeds, probably in a shroud (fragments of textile were recovered); moss had been laid over her head, knees and pelvis. Stakes and posts around the burial could be evidence that she was staked out on the foreshore, but were more likely markers for a mound of soil that was subsequently washed away by the tide. She had been killed by a violent blow to the head, possibly by a sword or axe; radiocarbon dating gives a date of 670–880. The second burial was also that of a woman, again laid from west to east, but she had been buried in a grave. Unfortunately we do not know whether these woman were locals or Viking attackers, and there has been speculation as to whether they had been murdered. It was common for burials to be interred on parish boundaries, and perhaps they were buried here specifically on the boundary between land and river but, if so, why were no more found? The position of the burials is sufficiently unusual to warrant speculation, and perhaps we might hypothesise that they were members of a Viking attacking force, killed on the foreshore and buried where they were killed.

There is an interesting parallel with the eleven burials found on the foreshore of the River Fleet in 1988. They were covered in stones and had probably been dismembered. Of these, eight have been studied: 3 males, 1 female and 4 adolescents. The pottery associated with them indicates a burial date between 1050 and 1100, and it has been suggested that these people were killed during the battle of London in 1066 when William I, having gained victory at Hastings, fought for the control of London (Mills 1996, 62).

The early port was probably little more than a foreshore or beach where boats could be pulled up, and produce sold from boats used as market stalls (Ayre *et al* in prep). Small timber trestles or boardwalks were found running out on to the foreshore, presumably for dry access to beached boats. Low banks of timber and gravel running towards the river across the foreshore may have been groynes to protect the beach.

Finds from the foreshore give us a picture of the trading taking place and the traders involved. There were three fine leather scabbards. The metalwork includes strap ends, such as a fine example decorated in the Trewhiddle style. It is squat, with an animal-head terminal. Another appears to be of Viking origin. There was a lead-alloy mount from a horse harness dating to the mid-tenth century, possibly also Viking in origin, and numerous coin brooches, probably also tenth-century, so called because either they were brooches made from coins or they used a disc of metal giving the impression of a coin (Fig. 5). They were made from copper alloy, pewter, silver or lead. The disc brooches were worn on the right shoulder by men and centrally by women. They have been found across Britain, Ireland and Sweden, and there are Merovingian examples, which suggests they were extremely popular throughout north-western Europe. (The

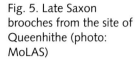

Fig. 5. Late Saxon brooches from the site of Queenhithe (photo: MoLAS)

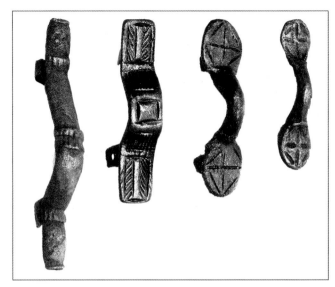

Merovingian empire of the Franks existed in Germany and France, and was replaced by the Carolingian dynasty in the eighth century.)

The pottery suggests a more limited range of influences with the majority being cooking pots made in the fabric known as Late Saxon Shelly ware, although Early Medieval Sandy ware is also relatively common, particularly in later tenth-century contexts. Imported pottery from other parts of England has been found, with by far the largest component being Ipswich Thetford-type ware which is found in London in the tenth century. Continental pottery was an unusual find and came exclusively from the Rhine Valley, including two Badorf amphorae for carrying wine.

The earliest revetments discovered on the foreshore date to some time after 970. They were low pile-and-plank revetments retaining a terrace of dry ground behind. The earliest, on the eastern side of the site, stood 0.6m high and was open to the trading shore of Queenhithe to the west. Although the central area was not excavated, a second, apparently different revetment was found to the west, standing to a similar height. The eastern edge was retained by timber stakes and a raft of logs was created over which rubble was laid. A line of posts in front may have been erected to prevent damage to boats and the revetment. Some 16m further east part of a reused Roman quay had been placed 14m south of the old Roman wall, and south of the quay a timber jetty about 2m by 2.5m was constructed.

At some time later the two terraces were combined to form one unit and were extended by about 2m into the river and over 3m to the west. There were other revetted terraces to the west, and an inlet lay between the two properties. This inlet was subsequently filled in and the quay extended southwards into the river. Exactly what function these terraces served is uncertain. Some of them could have been used for beaching boats and they would all have been covered at high tide. They no doubt prevented the foreshore being eroded and in some cases would have provided berthing points for trading vessels.

Fewer examples of continental metalwork were recovered from this phase of activity – either suggesting less continental trade, or reflecting the smaller areas excavated. The pottery was still dominated by locally produced wares but there was a steady and constant use of other English and continental material. The types of finds recovered were much more utilitarian in nature: the earliest phase produced such items as quernstones, a key, a fragment of rope, honestones and a spindle whorl, while the later phase produced such items as arrowheads and fish hooks.

There were major changes at the Queenhithe dock in the early years of the eleventh century: in 1026 a timber-laced platform was built eastwards from Queenhithe for a distance of 30m. It extended some 8m southwards into the river from the earlier revetment, and 2m west into the Hythe, producing a solid edge along the inlet. A second platform, dendrochronologically dated to 1045, was constructed with parallel, closely packed logs some 5m further out into the river.

These platforms no doubt fulfilled a series of functions, including prevention of erosion and flooding, and berthing for boats. However, the protruding logs and the silt washed between the logs made the platforms unsuitable for walking on, perhaps deliberately. The excavators believe that this was to force boats to use the Queenhithe dock where taxes would be paid and trade could be controlled. Similar timbers were found to the east but here timber pathways traversed the platforms from the river to individual properties, perhaps for personal access.

Billingsgate

The other early focus of the settlement lay in what is now the Billingsgate area near the site of London Bridge, around Fish Street Hill. In about AD 1000 a jetty, about 18m long, was constructed out into the river. It reused some of the old standing timbers from the Roman waterfront structures and added new ones to it to support a bank of ragstone, chalk and reused Roman building material laced together with interlocking tree branches. West of the jetty was a series of timber posts which coincided with a reduced level of the old Roman riverside wall and advanced about 13m further out into the river. Although the timbers were decayed at the top, there was evidence that planking had originally been laid along their top, so perhaps this structure formed a quay in front of the old river wall. The bank or jetty is thought to have been above water level at all times and the quay most of the time. Boats would have been able to moor against either of these and at low tide would have rested on the foreshore, allowing easy loading and unloading of cargo. The line of the jetty continued northwards beyond the river as a lane known as Rederesgate, a southward extension of Pudding Lane. Rederesgate means 'cattle gate', suggesting that livestock might have been unloaded here (Steedman *et al* 1992, 100–4).

In the early to mid-eleventh century new embankments were built further out into the river. These varied along the riverfront, reflecting the property divisions behind them, which indicates that they were built by individual tenement owners. The embankments commonly comprised vertical posts with branches and planks between, with alder roots and branches, and clay thrown in behind. The two earlier inlets were retained, both having gaps through the old riverside wall. One of these was narrowed to 5m and revetted with posts and planks to create a berthing area for boats to unload their cargo, which could then be carried straight up St Botolph's Lane (Steedman *et al* 1992, 104–6).

London Bridge

The earliest evidence for a post-Roman bridge at London comes from *ex situ* bridge timbers dating to *c.* 987–1032. Many northern European towns were building bridges at around this time to protect their rivers from marauding Viking ships and as an important means of communication. By the early eleventh century there was probably a defended settlement at the southern end of the bridge – the 'south work' or Southwark – which is mentioned in the great saga of St Olaf. A large ditch, some 4m wide and dating to the early eleventh century, has been found some 100m from the bridgehead in Southwark. In 1016 Cnut attacked London and apparently dug a channel around the southern bridgehead to take his boats around the defended bridge. No trace of this ditch has been found archaeologically but no doubt the Vikings would have part dragged their ships and part sailed them through the channels and creeks of low-lying Southwark (Watson *et al* 2001).

PALACES

There is no archaeological evidence for a royal palace or enclosure in the city during the middle and later Saxon periods although speculation has long suggested that there was one. Certainly by the mid-eleventh century Edward the Confessor had built himself a royal residence on Thorney Island at Westminster. Thorney Island was bounded by the Thames on its east side and by the River Tyburn, which flowed down from where Regent's Park now lies, on the other three sides. It has generally been accepted that the royal palace was founded there by Edward the Confessor when he began the rebuilding of the abbey in about 1050. However, the finding of timber foundations of a possible bridge crossing a wide timber-revetted ditch into the palace site, probably dating to the late tenth or early eleventh century, suggests an intriguing possibility: that there was occupation on the palace site before the reign of Edward the Confessor (Thomas *et al* in prep). No excavation has taken place within the inner part of the palace area to confirm this, and any occupation might not have been royal, but the existence of an earlier royal palace on the site must be considered a possibility.

RELIGION

Archaeological evidence for pre-Norman churches in the walled city is severely lacking. The cathedral of St Paul was founded in AD 604 but no archaeological trace has been recovered. The cathedral and its successors were, no doubt, the most imposing buildings in London and the later versions were probably the only ones in stone. A few parish churches have a strong claim for Late Saxon foundations, notably All Hallows by the Tower and St Peter Cornhill. A Late Saxon date has also been suggested for St Alban Wood Street (Vince 1990).

Excavations at the site of St Lawrence Jewry did provide evidence, however, that this church just predates the Norman Conquest. It lay on the west side of Lawrence Lane, probably below where the current church now stands. To the north was its burial ground, surrounded by a fence, in which eighteen burials have been defined as coming from this early phase. Many of the coffins survived, rudimentarily made by fixing boards together often with no head or foot board. Two have been dendrochronologically dated to 1046 and 1066 respectively. Thirteen of these burials were adults and six had stone pillows under the head or feet or on either side of the head. Five had twigs (probably hazel) buried alongside them, a peculiar burial ritual seen throughout the medieval period (Bateman 2000, 46–50).

One other structure is highly suggestive of ecclesiastical building. Contained in the waterfront structures at Queenhithe were six remarkable pieces of reused timber from an arcaded tenth-century timber building (Ayre *et al* in prep). The first, found in 1991, was a sculpted oak building post with an unusual form of arcading springing from it. The remainder were found in 1995 reused in later revetments. They included three large sculpted oak arcade posts and one similar but smaller post. The smaller post had a simple splice joint cut in its base, showing that originally it must have joined a vertical timber beneath it. The final piece was a Y-shaped oak timber with a protruding boss. The dendrochronological dates for the timbers all overlapped and they are interpreted as having come from a single building. It was probably double aisled and the three types of arcade structure may have been used one above the other (for which there was also jointing evidence) giving a minimum height of 8.4m. A suggested reconstruction of the building is shown in Fig. 6.

The triple-level arcade may have existed for the entire length of the building, which would indicate a large and very high-status hall, or perhaps it was used in just one location, which suggests a tower, possibly of a church. Aisled halls are extremely rare for a tenth-century building and are confined, so far as is known, only to royal palaces. The ash pegs found in the timbers suggest that they were fastenings for horizontal beams, a technique seen in Norwegian stave churches. The decoration is not dissimilar to the stone tower of the church at Barton-on-Humber and thus the current interpretation is that they came from a church probably situated close to Queenhithe and dating to the tenth century.

Fig. 6. Reconstruction of an aisled hall from timbers found at Queenhithe (photo: MoLAS)

Two Saxon monastic foundations are known from the London area: east of the River Lea at Barking and at Westminster. The origins of Westminster Abbey are steeped in legend and confused by the fabrication of charters by monks in the eleventh and twelfth centuries (Brooke and Keir 1975, 195). It lay on Thorney Island to the west of the site of the palace on the highest ground, suggesting that its origins are earlier than those of the palace. A minster church was probably founded there in the eighth and ninth centuries; a Benedictine monastery was certainly founded there by St Dunstan, Archbishop of Canterbury, on land granted by King Edgar, sometime between 959 and 972. Of these buildings nothing has ever been recorded archaeologically. Edward the Confessor certainly rebuilt the abbey, and resided in a palace there by the end of his reign in 1065. Foundations of the nave arcade to the abbey beneath the current nave indicate a nave of twelve bays with transepts and an eastern apse. This was almost certainly by far the largest building of its date in England and was influenced by the abbey at Jumieges in Normandy where Edward had lived in exile. Such a building would have been an enormously impressive structure to Londoners primarily used to timber buildings and certainly not aware of the architectural and stylistic advances on the continent. Fragments of the original floor laid in large tiles 25cm across were also found (Tanner and Clapham 1935).

A large ditch was dug in the 1050s on the south side of the abbey, perhaps as a boundary, cutting through deep layers of fluvial sediments of similar date which suggests that the whole area upon which the abbey was built was flooded at this time (Thomas *et al* in prep). A gravel road laid over these silts may have provided access within the precinct during construction works. The backfills of the ditch contained large quantities of pottery which show the transition between Late Saxon wares and new types just coming into production (Mills 1995; Goffin in Mills 1995).

CONCLUSION: LONDON AT THE NORMAN CONQUEST

It now seems clear that when Alfred refounded the city in the late ninth century the settlement was small and possibly had two foci. One lay around Queenhithe with a grid of two streets running north from it up to Cheapside. The other, which probably dates to the late tenth century, lay around the bridgehead at the base of Fish Street Hill, with a similar grid of streets running north, perhaps to modern Eastcheap or Fenchurch Street. Churches of the late ninth and tenth centuries were probably confined to these areas, although there is evidence that All Hallows by the Tower and St Peter Cornhill have Saxon origins. There was certainly a cathedral in the city, since documentary evidence suggests that there had been one since the seventh century. It has also been suggested that there was a royal house on the site of the Roman Cripplegate fort, in the north-west corner, but so far there is no archaeological evidence for this.

Importantly the initial settlement areas were around the dock at Queenhithe and the jetty to the east by the bridgehead. Both of these areas were developed to take the trade that was vital to London's success. During the tenth century the settlement expanded with the filling in of streets within the existing grid and development along Cheapside as far as the Walbrook. That grid was then carried northwards on the other side of Cheapside in about AD 1000 in a pattern which mirrored that of the streets south of Cheapside. This expansion of the city can be seen where Bow Lane was extended northwards to become Lawrence Lane, which was eventually extended to the site of the later Guildhall. This growth away from the river may also have occurred at the eastern part of the settlement by the bridgehead, with streets developing north from Eastcheap to Fenchurch Street. Throughout this period some of the old Roman routes through the city must still have operated, and the walls and gates around the city still stood, defining its limits.

The overwhelming majority of the houses found were fairly rudimentary, either ground-level or sunken-floored buildings, constructed of timber and wattle. Often small animal enclosures and industrial workshops were associated with the houses. Their occupants were probably craftspeople and traders, and partly self-sufficient. The development of a market west of the Walbrook suggests people were creating enough wares for sale and that Londoners had enough money to buy some goods imported from elsewhere in England and from the continent. High-status buildings were very rare, with perhaps only the timbers from the aisled hall indicating any structure that was not domestic. The siting of a royal house is still uncertain, but any such buildings would only have formed part-time accommodation for the king since at this time Winchester retained an important place as a royal and administrative centre.

At the Norman Conquest London was a sufficiently thriving and prosperous settlement for William I to consider it a vital place to conquer. Whether the burials on the shore of the Fleet were victims of the battle for London or not, the documents testify to the hard-fought struggle that ensued. William also saw the importance of emphasising his legitimacy by following his predecessor, Harold II, and having himself crowned in Edward the Confessor's abbey, thus cementing its place as the royal coronation church and setting in motion Westminster's rise to political pre-eminence.

CHAPTER 2

London, 1066–1200

INTRODUCTION

The Norman Conquest does not reveal itself to any great extent in the archaeological record. Apart from the skeletons recovered from the foreshore, mentioned in the previous chapter, as perhaps being casualties of the battle of London, without historical evidence we would not know that a significant event had occurred in 1066. Early Norman houses were still built of timber, often wattle and daub, and some continued to be built as sunken structures. The clear change occurs in the later eleventh and twelfth centuries when there was major development and expansion of the city. New streets were laid out and previously unoccupied areas built upon. A significant number of new parish churches appeared in the later eleventh and twelfth centuries, usually built in stone, and the first stone houses emerged soon after in the twelfth century. These signify a distinct change from the London of the tenth century. The most obvious and significant influence of the new Norman conquerors was the castles built at either end of the city: the Tower of London to the east and Baynard's Castle and Montfichet's Tower to the west.

The lifestyle of most Londoners changed little in the early part of this period but the increase in wealth probably led to a higher standard of living. This increase in wealth was a result of the increase in trade, and this led to the expansion of the docks.

Monastic houses were attracted to the burgeoning city in the twelfth century, both inside and outside its walls, and the settlement expanded around them along the main streets out of the city.

Westminster Palace was an important site from Edward the Confessor's time but was still one of many royal houses. The only permanent government institution, the exchequer or treasury, remained at Winchester until the later twelfth century, in the reign of Henry II, when it moved to Westminster.

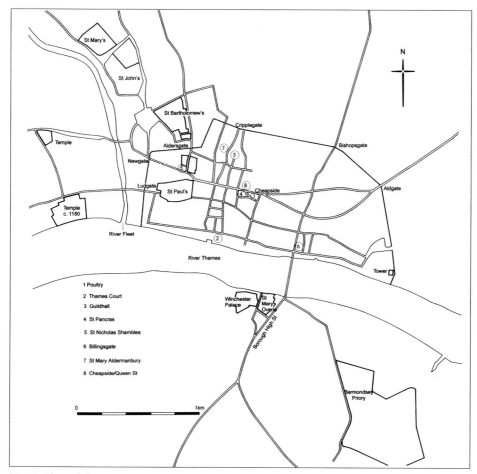

Fig. 7. Plan of the city 1066–1200

LAYOUT AND DEVELOPMENT

The latter part of the eleventh century saw the continued expansion of the network of streets that had already been established, but this was much enhanced during the twelfth century which was the formative period for the laying out of the street pattern (Fig. 7). Thames Street was created in the twelfth century as a means of access to the increasingly developed dockside at Queenhithe, Vintry, Dowgate and Billingsgate, and followed the course of the old Roman riverside wall (Dyson in Steedman, Dyson and Schofield 1992, 128–31). This made it easier to get from one wharf or property to another without having to travel all the way up to Cheapside. This of course encouraged the laying of new lanes down to the dockside areas as access was now much more easy. For instance, Bull Wharf Lane became a thoroughfare, probably in the

1160s, and was known as Dibeleslane, but its line harks back to the Alfredian reoccupation of the city when it formed the centre line of the reoccupied area. It clearly became a lane after the construction of Thames Street in the late eleventh or early twelfth century since, although earlier streets crossed this line, Bull Wharf Lane stopped at Thames Street.

The siting of the parish churches is a good indicator of the density of occupation and these clearly suggest a strong focus towards the dockside areas, Cheapside and the streets laid out in the eleventh century. Few were sited in the eastern part of the city (Keene in Palliser 2000, 192). Indeed, the north-eastern part of the city seems, like its Roman counterpart, to have been fairly undeveloped in the eleventh and twelfth centuries. Indeed, this was true to such an extent that trenches were dug during the twelfth century to rob out the Roman walls that may still have been standing there. This is especially true of the area east of Bishopsgate and Gracechurch Street. This lack of early development allowed new monastic houses (which needed plenty of space for their precincts) to be sited there in the twelfth and thirteenth centuries.

Medieval Southwark, like its Roman predecessor, was the principal suburb of London. It lay in the diocese of Winchester and was reached from London across London Bridge and from the south along the old Roman Watling Street which led to Kent. The settlement was based around Borough High Street which led southwards from London Bridge.

Efforts to reclaim and retain the southern foreshore upstream of London Bridge seem to have been made in the later eleventh century, probably as a response to the catastrophic effects of flooding (Watson *et al* 2001). One revetment contained timbers dating to 1081–2. Further attempts included a revetment structure with a tie-back or front brace and layers of brushwood and branches, which dated to 1095. The fragmentary nature of these revetments and their regular replacement indicate the frequency with which they were eroded and damaged by the river. The *Anglo-Saxon Chronicle* describes how the bridge was washed away in 1097, and one revetment comprising a tie-back and stakes has actually been dated to that year: it was presumably built as a replacement after the flooding described in the *Chronicle*.

Repeated attempts were made to retain the foreshore but a change is apparent during the twelfth century when, upstream of the bridge, a series of timber groynes was built out into the river to prevent further erosion of the banks and foreshore. The area downstream of London Bridge is less well understood but the indications are that this area was better protected from the effects of the river by the bridge and therefore the revetments were longer lasting and the builders were able to extend further out into the river, thus reclaiming more land. One of these revetments contained timber dendrochronologically dated to 1197 and consisted of baseplates held in place by stakes with timber posts inserted into them. The posts probably retained horizontal planks similar to those found at Billingsgate on the north side of the river.

The western suburb along Fleet Street has not had the extensive excavations that have been undertaken over most of the rest of the city and is therefore less well understood. It certainly became the site of some of the finest houses in the country but at this period it was sufficiently underdeveloped to allow the siting of the Knights Templar House and, later, the Carmelite Friars House. The siting of parish churches at St Bride's along Fleet Street and St Andrew's along Holborn does, however, indicate communities dwelling there, although St Bride's is undoubtedly pre-Conquest in origin.

The north-western suburb, as we shall see, became a focus for religious communities at an early date. That some of these, such as St Bartholomew's, were set back from the street suggests that there was already housing stretching out from the city walls in the first quarter of the twelfth century. It was based around the streets of Aldersgate and St John Street.

The later development of the northern suburb along the old Roman road of what is now Bishopsgate was a consequence of the later development of the north-eastern corner of the city and this meant that there was less need for extra-mural settlement. Much of the land comprised open fields, owned by the Bishop of London. During the twelfth century cottages were probably built on the eastern side of Bishopsgate, although no buildings have been discovered. The western side was probably marshland in the Walbrook Valley. Behind the cottages on the east side lay gardens which were used for growing food and contained wells lined with timber. Beyond these properties lay the open fields which were extensively quarried for their brickearth, used to make tiles (and, later, bricks) and gravel for paths and roads. Alongside the road lay what may have been a water-supply system, consisting of parallel ditches interspersed with large settling tanks, lined with stake and wattle fences. The purity of the water must be questioned, however, as the ditches contained cattle horn cores, flax waste and the skeleton of a dead dog (Thomas *et al* 1997, 15–19).

HOUSES

The timber buildings of the early eleventh century were replaced in most areas during the latter part of the century and new housing was built along the extended grid network of streets. The early buildings at the junction of Watling Street, Bow Lane and Basing Lane from the post-1050 period were very similar to those of the later Saxon period, indicating a continuity in style and building technique. Four sunken-floored buildings lay behind the Bow Lane frontage and may have coexisted with buildings along the street front. One large building was 12.7m long, over 5.6m wide and more than 0.7m deep below the contemporary ground surface. Its walls comprised planks supported by posts with the south wall consisting of a double wall of planks, presumably for added strength along its longest wall. A second large structure of similar size also had a double line of planks along its longest wall. The floors were of beaten earth and timber. The pits behind the Bow Lane frontage were predominantly cesspits, sometimes wattle lined, presumably serving the houses along the street, and there were at least two barrel-lined wells (Schofield et al 1990, 48–9).

At Milk Street, no timber buildings from the second half of the eleventh century were recovered but this was probably due to destruction from later stone buildings. The preponderance of pits behind the Milk Street frontage and the almost total absence along the street indeed suggests that there were originally timber structures here. As found on Bow Lane, timber-lined cesspits appeared for the first time during this period. The finds assemblages from the extensive pits included more ceramic crucibles, pigment (again probably madder as in the previous period), bone mounts, leather waste and an axe (Schofield et al 1990, 117–18). This might suggest that the buildings along the streets were used by artisans practising a variety of crafts to produce goods to sell either in their own shops or perhaps in local markets. Indeed, practice designs for metal objects, perhaps brooches, were found inscribed on bone motif-pieces, suggesting metalworking in the area, and two of the crucibles had fragments of silver in them (Schofield et al 1990, 176).

The later eleventh and twelfth centuries saw not only the expansion of the settlement area within the city but also the emergence of stone dwellings. On the corner of Cheapside and Queen Street lay a cellar built from ragstone and tile with a set of steps, 1.5m wide, entering the cellar to the south. The floor of the cellar was about 0.70m below the contemporary ground surface. The cellar measured at least 3m by 3.5m and was perhaps designed for storage. It appears to have been constructed in the second half of the twelfth century and not to have gone out of use until the late thirteenth century (Hill and Woodger 1999, 42–4). Another cellar was constructed from beech piles which presumably were the foundations for a masonry wall that had subsequently been destroyed. Only the east wall was found, and dendrochronological dating of the timbers suggests they were felled in 1091, which means that currently they are the earliest dated beech timbers in London. In the area outside the cellar and the building was an open space used for the digging of rubbish pits. Three of the pits were wattle-lined cesspits up to 1.5m deep and up to 4m long. The size of these pits suggests that they might have been used by multiple occupants; they were dated to the second half of the eleventh and the twelfth centuries.

During the twelfth century stone-founded buildings began to be constructed along Bow Lane. In the open space behind them, large cesspits and a barrel-lined well were dug. One of the stone-founded buildings, probably measuring about 6m square, fronted on to Basing Lane to the south (Schofield *et al* 1990, 49–52). New stone buildings were also constructed in the twelfth century at Well Court. One fronted on to Bow Lane and consisted of two cellars in total measuring 19.4m by perhaps 10m. The substantial chalk walls were about 1.5m thick. A smaller wall continued eastwards, indicating that the structure extended further at ground-floor level. Both cellars had brickearth floors. The area to the north contained pits, which may mean that the building formerly on the site had been demolished and it was now an open yard (Schofield *et al* 1990, 82). At Milk Street the new buildings were again in stone but the finds from the pits suggest continuity of use (Fig. 8). One house, measuring about 10m by 7m, fronted on to the street. Parts of a second stone building, probably of at least two rooms with cellars with brickearth and clay floors, were found to the north. Once again the pits contained crucibles and pigment as well as leather shoes, silk thread, wooden and glass vessels, a bone needle case and an iron padlock (Schofield *et al* 1990, 118–24).

The use of stone in these buildings was probably confined to the cellars and foundations, with the superstructure still built in timber. This made the houses more durable, and new timber-building techniques allowed the buildings to be built much higher, probably to two or three storeys. Many of the buildings had a cellar, although this might not have covered the whole extent of the building and was often used just for storage. These houses were often divided both horizontally and vertically, with numerous families dwelling in them (Keene in Palliser 2000, 194). Many were used by artisans or contained shops at ground-floor level with accommodation above. There seems, for instance, to have been a group of metalworkers along Milk Street and the pigment recovered may also suggest dyers were present; no doubt groups of artisans and shopkeepers practising similar trades came together in many districts of the city.

The earliest stone building behind the river frontage at the Queenhithe dock dated to the early twelfth century and reused the stone dock walls as the western

Fig. 8. Twelfth-century houses at Milk Street (photo: Museum of London)

and southern walls of the building (Ayre *et al* in prep). The east wall was built on timber piles to prevent the building subsiding into the boggy ground beneath. The only surviving archaeological feature within this building at this date was a large hearth or fireplace. Attached to the outside of the south wall of the building was a garderobe pit constructed from timber posts in the corners with horizontal planks between. A later alteration to the building was the insertion of a cellar which removed almost all of the earlier deposits. A barrel to collect water was set into the timber floor of the cellar and drains flowed into it. The eastern wall of the cellar was formed by timber staves. The cellar was subsequently rebuilt, the barrel backfilled and the drains robbed out. The east wall was rebuilt as two stave walls with clay between, perhaps to keep water out. New drains were laid, running into another barrel, which dendro-chronological dates suggest were inserted in the 1120s. By the end of the twelfth century a new floor of timber joists had been made and the cellar narrowed on the eastern side to make way for the new Bull Wharf Lane.

The stone from these buildings would most probably have comprised Caen stone from Normandy, chalk from the South or North Downs, ragstone from Kent and greensand from the Reigate area of Surrey. The commonest form of roof covering was probably thatch, although timber and straw were also used. Ceramic tiles were introduced at this time but none of these was found in the Cheapside area prior to the mid-twelfth century, suggesting that they were not introduced widely until then (Betts in Schofield *et al* 1990, 221–5; Keilly in Egan *et al* 1998, 26). Wooden shingles also appeared at around this time but these rarely survive. Slate is thought to have been first employed in London for roofing towards the end of the twelfth century. Few houses would have had glass in their windows. Early medieval glass does not survive well but is found so rarely that it seems likely that most houses had only shutters on their windows.

Daily Life

The diet and lifestyle of most Londoners probably changed little in the later eleventh and early twelfth centuries. The network of food distribution which appeared in the thirteenth and fourteenth centuries may have only been in its infancy in the twelfth century and many householders probably owned a few poultry and other animals, perhaps pigs, for their meat. No doubt they bought their other food from markets but there was not the emphasis on the cash economy that there was in later years.

Fig. 9. A musical horn found at No. 1 Poultry (photo: MoLAS)

The artefactual and environmental material discarded around the late eleventh-century revetments in Southwark suggests that the local inhabitants used mostly local handmade cooking pots, and that people were throwing away hay or animal fodder – the waste from the processing of cereal crops. Their food remains include bones from cattle and sheep, chicken, goose and fish such as cod and whiting. Many utensils would have been fairly simple – wood and horn were popular materials. The use of these materials even extended as far as musical instruments as demonstrated by a horn found at No.1 Poultry (Fig. 9).

New ceramic types appeared in the twelfth century, most notably South Hertfordshire greyware and London ware. Imported material is less common from twelfth-century deposits as are high-quality goods, suggesting greater reliance on locally produced, cheaper products.

MARKETS

The main market for London seems to have been in the Cheapside area and, as we have seen, there was already a market established behind the frontage in the Late Saxon period. Evidence from the Poultry site in the city suggests that life did not change that much in the early Norman period. However, the shops around the market space were replaced by a terrace of buildings, perhaps used as workshops (Fig. 10). The buildings were of timber with posts set into the ground and with earth or mortar floors. There was widespread evidence of iron- and boneworking being carried out in these buildings. The main change was the expansion into the undeveloped space behind the buildings along Bucklersbury

Fig. 10. Reconstruction painting of No. 1 Poultry

during the twelfth century. Here new timber buildings were constructed with their own back yards divided by fences (Rowsome 2000, 50–3).

Other markets sprang up in London during the twelfth century. The buildings on the eastern side of Lawrence Lane, immediately to the south of the present Guildhall, were demolished to make way for an open market containing temporary buildings and over forty ovens and hearths for cooking. Waste pits lined in wattle were also found in the area (Fig. 11). The demolition of these buildings confirms other evidence for a decline in Scandinavian trade in London at this time (Bateman 2000, 58). The earliest reference to what may perhaps have been a Guildhall dates to 1128 and concerns a plot of land leased to the 'Gialla'.

Defences

The city defences were still primarily those of the Roman period: the old Roman walls which surrounded the city on its northern, eastern and western sides. The wall at this time had six main gates: Ludgate, Newgate, Aldersgate, Cripplegate, Bishopsgate and Aldgate, plus a postern gate by the Tower. This

Fig. 11. A wattle-lined pit from the Guildhall Yard (photo: MoLAS)

postern gate, built before 1190, was excavated in the 1970s and can still be seen in the underpass near the Tower. In addition to the walls, castles were added at both ends of the river to strengthen the city's defences.

DOCKS AND LONDON BRIDGE

Billingsgate

The initial post-Conquest waterfront activity demonstrates a continuity which, like the activity away from the river, bears no relation to the change in royal and political regime. Indeed, at Billingsgate alterations to either decayed or disused structures can only be dated to about 1050–70 and may indeed have occurred before the Conquest. During the twelfth century other alterations were carried out, including the construction of a timber-planked walkway and consolidation of the bank with revetments, although it is clear that this would have been under water at high tide. New revetments actually began to reclaim land from the river and the western inlet was infilled to create a unified frontage along the river. The revetments consisted of vertically driven piles with planks between and gently sloping ground behind. The tops of the revetments were not above high tide and thus allowed more silt to accumulate gradually behind them. Areas of hard standing lay at the top of the slope beyond the reach of the river. Posts, perhaps mooring posts, were found further out into the river (Steedman *et al* 1992).

Queenhithe

A new chalk and ragstone wall was built as the east side of the Queenhithe dock in the early twelfth century; the timbers in its core were dendrochronologically dated to 1103. The wall formed the river frontage along the Thames as well as the quayside, as its top was well above the level of the river (Ayre *et al* in prep).

Development of the Thames foreshore was carried out in piecemeal fashion. On the eastern side, posts aligned north–south with a return to the west at the river end were all that remained of a timber revetment. The posts were clearly designed to be covered at high tide as their tops would have been some 0.9m below the water at high tide and about 0.8m above the water level at low tide. This suggests that the posts were designed to support barges which floated on to them at high tide. There was an inlet here bounded by the posts, plus a brushwood platform and a timber walkway within the inlet. This walkway was on the line of the later Bull Wharf Lane, suggesting that the lane originated as a public path through an inlet to the river. A further stave-built structure may have been part of a set of steps leading down to the foreshore at the edge of the Queenhithe dock. Along the foreshore itself a large area was covered with a layer of cobbles as an area for beaching boats.

A major change to the waterfront at Queenhithe can be dated precisely by dendrochronology to 1121. This appears to have been the beginning of the period of major reclamation with increasing areas of the river taken over for dry land. Initially, a timber baseplate was cut into the cobbled foreshore, some 4.5m out from the former riverfront, and vertical staves were inserted into a groove down its centre presenting a solid wall against the river, over 2m high. These staves were supported by tie-backs on the landward side and material was thrown in behind the revetment. The land behind was open space initially, containing a large number of hearths. These were simple structures with brickearth bases. An archaeomagnetic date from one hearth indicated its last firing to have taken place between 1120 and 1130. These simple structures may have been used as cook shops.

Between 1132 and 1157 (most probably in the 1130s), a new stave revetment was built forming the eastern side of the dock and widening it. This lay at a somewhat higher level, indicating that boats would only have been able to enter this side of the dock at high tide and that larger boats might have had to moor outside the dock altogether (Fig. 12).

In the early 1140s there was a major fire at Queenhithe which burned the tops of the revetments and doubtless destroyed timber buildings in the vicinity. The riverfront was rebuilt in 1145–7, in the form of a new revetment reclaiming much more of the river. Revetments to the south of one property, to the west of an inlet, advanced dry land by 9m, with revetments built on three sides to the south of the old waterfront. They were constructed from earthfast oak posts with horizontal oak planks between them; horizontal layers of five planks still survived. Tie-backs were constructed on the inside of the structure to hold it firmly in place and the new space within the revetments was filled with huge amounts of dumped material. On the other, eastern, side of the inlet was another post and plank revetment. The inlet itself was 9m long and 2.5m wide and would have been large enough to contain a small boat such as a lighter. Shortly

Fig. 12. Twelfth-century revetments at Queenhithe (photo: MoLAS)

afterwards, in around 1151, the revetment forming the western side of the inlet was taken down, and the inlet was blocked with timbers and infilled.

At about the same time the eastern edge of Queenhithe was extended into the river by a further 5.5m using timbers which also dated to 1145–7, suggesting that they may have been reused from the dismantled inlet revetment. This new structure was built on three sides with posts and planks, just as the revetments by the inlet had been.

Less than twenty years later, between 1165 and 1170, yet another revetment was built about 6m further south. It too was a post and plank structure and, significantly, had braces to support it on the river side, indicating that vessels were not intended to moor against the structure. There was also evidence that the eastern side of the Queenhithe dock was reclaimed and became a new property, thus narrowing the old dock, perhaps suggesting that its importance was in decline.

In total, then, about 29m of riverfront were reclaimed in the area of the Queenhithe during the twelfth century, compared to the 29–40m of reclamation immediately to its east at Vintner's Place. Such reclamation was carried out because the revetments needed replacing on a regular basis, perhaps every twenty or thirty years. This was possibly exacerbated by the rising river levels and because the increased trade and wealth in London meant that there was a need for more space for trading and occupation.

London Bridge

London's only river crossing was London Bridge. Evidence for its rebuilding on the southern side of the Thames consisted of a large oak baseplate, possibly forming part of a bridge abutment, which came from a tree felled after 1056. Two sets of slots in the timber were for posts, the outer perhaps for securing the structure to the land and the inner for the upper parts of the bridge. If so these would give a roadway dimension for the bridge of about 4.6m, wide enough for carts to pass one another. The upstream side of the bridge was protected by a series of revetments dating to about 1080–1100 (Watson et al 2001).

During the second half of the twelfth century there were again major works on the bridge. Between 1158 and 1170 a caisson, a supported trench dug into the river for a bridge pier, was built. The four sides were constructed in timber with the landward side being cut into the existing foreshore. The caisson was perhaps then filled with rubble or soil to support the main bridge structure above. A second caisson, measuring about 5m by 6m, was built on top of the first, perhaps between 1160 and 1168. It included a lot of earlier wood which

Fig. 13. Reconstruction painting of London Bridge

may have been reused from the original caisson. This could be the work on the timber bridge that Peter de Colechurch is documented as rebuilding in 1163.

In about 1176 construction began on a new bridge in stone, supervised by Peter de Colechurch and completed in 1209. This was one of London's most famous landmarks and survived in much the same form up until the nineteenth century (Fig. 13). The bridge was probably funded by Henry II, the Archbishop of Canterbury, a visiting papal legate and the first mayor, Henry Fitz Ailwyn. In the centre of the bridge was a chapel dedicated to St Thomas Becket (murdered in 1170), where Peter de Colechurch was later buried. This certainly was not the earliest stone bridge in the area: one had been built between 1100 and 1135 over the River Lea, the boundary between historic Middlesex and Essex, at the behest of Queen Maud, but London Bridge was certainly on a scale not seen in England before. It was about 276m long and was supported by nineteen piers. There were nineteen stone arches and a drawbridge in the centre. The width of the bridge is not certain but it was variously described as being between about

7.5m and 9.5m although, of course, the roadway became much narrower as houses were built on either side. The road itself may only have been 3.5–4.5m in width but was certainly wide enough for carts to pass one another.

The mode of construction is uncertain but it has been suggested that piling engines, mounted on barges, drove timber piles into the river bed to form a structure into which rubble could be dumped to create a working platform for the stone piers above the river level. Clearly high tides would have seriously restricted the times when construction could have occurred. Each stone pier had a cutwater to protect it from floods and a boat-shaped timber starling built of elm to protect it from the river. The bridge was sited where the timber bridge had been and the approach roads remained in the same place; the bridge may have been constructed one arch at a time so that each could be fitted to the existing timber bridge to keep it operational for some months of the year. Neither the piers nor the arches were consistent in size: the piers varied from 4.6m to 10.7m across, although most were about 6.5m. A large central pier was built to house the chapel to St Thomas.

At the southern end of the bridge, the ground level was consolidated and the old timber caissons were dismantled. Timber piles, of which at least two were iron-shod, were driven into the ground. Oak sill beams were then laid and these were founded on beech piles. The sill beams were halved oak logs about 0.60m in diameter and one was 6.35m long. The dendrochronological dates indicate that the timbers were felled in 1187 or 1188. On top of these sill beams the ashlar walls of the piers were built. The stones mostly derived from Purbeck and Kentish ragstone and were fixed in place with iron clamps. This southern abutment was then filled with ragstone and chalk but was left open on its southern side to create an access ramp. The abutment was some 11m long and 19m wide and would have stood to a height of 4.5m.

Clearly this 33-year construction was a major feat of engineering; nothing of this scale in bridge-building terms had ever been attempted in England before. It was also an extremely important structure. At last it provided secure, stable and permanent access from London across to its neighbour Southwark – although, as we shall see, it was not without its structural problems.

PALACES

Winchester Palace

The rise in wealth and importance of London in the late eleventh and early twelfth centuries, and the increasing use of the royal palace at Westminster, led to nobles and bishops wanting to have London residences. Most of these appeared in the later twelfth century, or more often in the thirteenth century, when both London and Westminster became more of a focus for political and economic affairs in England. One, however, was founded in the 1140s by the Bishop of Winchester, to the west of London Bridge in Southwark, adjacent to the Priory of St Mary Overie (now Southwark Cathedral). Henry of Blois, the immensely powerful Bishop of Winchester and brother of King Stephen, acquired lands in Southwark for his house from Orgar the Rich in 1144–9.

At about this time Orgar's house was demolished to make way for a structure which is thought to have been part of the bishop's new house (Seeley in prep). This new building was large, some 20m long and probably 8.4m wide, and laid parallel to the river. It was divided into two rooms of which the eastern had a sleeper wall down its centre – presumably to support columns and a vault and perhaps an upper floor. The foundations were largely of chalk and gravel. Two L-shaped foundations to the north may have supported a staircase. This building was extended eastwards but slightly offset to the north by 1.75m, and there was evidence of another extension to the building to the south. The eastern extension used high-status greensand quoins at one corner. An upper floor may have been used as the principal accommodation. Use of the upstairs as the main sleeping and dining space tends to become standard practice in high-status residences in the second half of the twelfth century, making this potentially an early example. Land to the south and east of this building was enclosed by a stone wall. The remains of part of another building close to the main one comprised ashlar-faced walls with rubble behind. This was, perhaps, the Bishop of Winchester's private chapel.

Gravel surfaces and levelling layers were dumped to the north over the earlier building towards the riverfront. These were clearly dumped to level out the ground after more than 2m of deposits had been eroded, probably during the second half of the twelfth century. It is unclear what caused this enormous erosion in north Southwark. There seems no reason (nor evidence) to believe that it was deliberate and so perhaps it was caused by a period of very heavy flooding brought on by the rise in the river owing to the construction of the stone London Bridge in the 1170s and 1180s. The earliest waterfront found in the Winchester Palace area extended at least 40m west of the St Mary Overie dock. Horizontal beech planks were found behind vertical posts which were dendrochronologically dated to between 1191 and 1209. The date of 1191 is interesting as it accords well with the known revetments constructed at Queenhithe and Westminster only ten or so years earlier when the substantial rise in river level occurred. Perhaps, then, these revetments were built after a period of disastrous flooding had caused serious damage to the area, in order to prevent a repeat of such an occurrence.

Tower of London

Two royal palaces were sited in London at this time. One was the defensive fortress at the Tower of London on the east side of the city and the other was the Palace of Westminster. It is believed that William the Conqueror built a temporary fortress on the site of the Tower early in his reign as a symbol of the power of the new Norman monarchy and to dissuade any of his new subjects from rebellion (Parnell 1983, 107). Evidence for this stronghold takes the form of a large ditch which runs from north-east to south-west to the north of the later White Tower and returns southwards towards the river at its western end. The ditch was some 8m wide and 3.5m deep, more than sufficient for a defensive ditch (Parnell 1983, 118). In the 1080s William had Gundulf, Bishop of Rochester, build him his new stone keep, the White Tower, which doubtless lay within an enclosure or bailey. This keep, still one of the largest and best preserved of all Norman keeps, was originally entered at first-floor level and contains the beautiful chapel of St John within its walls. At this time the Tower lay within the circuit of the Roman city walls and continued to do so throughout the eleventh and twelfth centuries. In the thirteenth century the Tower was extended and the old city walls demolished. Only very meagre evidence survives of the activities at the Tower until the end of the twelfth century when Richard I had the defences around the White Tower substantially developed. The earlier ditch to the north of the White Tower was redug and extended westwards towards the Beauchamp Tower from where it is thought to have turned southwards to the Bell Tower. This tower and the curtain wall along the south side of the inner ward are also thought to date from this period (Parnell 1983, 109).

Palace of Westminster

The Palace of Westminster upon Thorney Island lay immediately to the east of the abbey (Fig. 14). It was built on a spur of land which jutted out into the River Thames (Thomas *et al* in prep). At this time the English kings were peripatetic; that is, they moved around the country ruling from wherever they happened to be. The three principal royal palaces were at Westminster, Gloucester and Winchester, the old Saxon capital. The exchequer was the only static item of government and that remained at Winchester until late in the twelfth century

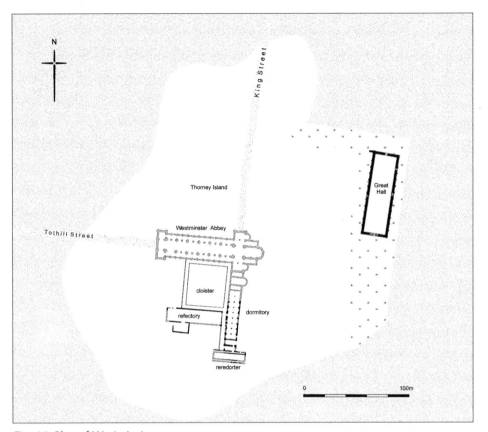

Fig. 14. Plan of Westminster

when Henry II built a new building known as the 'receipt of the exchequer' at Westminster. The palace was one of many royal houses but progressively became the main seat of the monarch. In 1097 William Rufus had built the colossal Great Hall (now known as Westminster Hall). This measured some 73m by 20.5m internally, making it the largest stone hall north of the Alps, and it is now the largest surviving in Europe. Excavations in the 1830s revealed that it had an earth floor but no evidence was found to indicate the original supports for the roof. There has been much speculation as to whether it had two rows of supports, one row of supports or indeed none. It seems unlikely that technology at the time would have allowed the builders to span the building without pillars and probable that there were two rows of timber posts, which made it a three-aisled building with the central aisle leading down to the royal throne set on a dais at the south end. There was a fine arcade around the inside with a walkway behind, allowing access around the inside of the building at window level. The Great Hall was used for major state occasions such as coronations and feasts.

The now destroyed lesser hall where the monarch ate and carried out his daily business may originally have been Edward the Confessor's hall and it lay to the south in the residential part of the palace. It was initially a single-storey building with a 'screens passage' across its northern end to divide the eating space from the place where the food was prepared. Henry II added a second storey in the twelfth century, and from this time onwards all of the principal rooms were at first-floor level. It had windows with the characteristic chevron moulding common in the second half of the twelfth century. A grand royal chamber, known in later periods as the Painted Chamber, projected out from this dining hall towards the river at the south end, and there was probably a chapel dedicated to St Stephen also projecting out towards the river at the north end of the hall. This was rebuilt in the thirteenth century.

Higher river levels caused by rising sea level and the dam effect of the narrow arches of London Bridge necessitated the construction of a river wall around the palace and abbey in 1179–81. A document refers to the 'quay' being built by Ailnoth the engineer at this date and radiocarbon dates from timbers are consistent with this (Colvin *et al* 1963, 493; Thomas *et al* in prep). The abbey walls can still be seen on Abingdon Street to a complete height of about 8.5m and set into the wall was the outlet for the great drain from the abbey latrine. The palace's river walls now only survive beneath the ground but their plan can be reconstructed from where they have been excavated. These walls returned westwards towards the abbey at the south end of the palace and westwards towards the old medieval road of King Street, north of where Big Ben now stands. Here a large dock was built to unload barges. The dock had a timber floor which was covered at high tide so that boats could sail on to it and was exposed at low tide so that these flat-bottomed boats could rest on the floor and be unloaded. The dock was at least 13m long and perhaps extended up to a building to the west making it 51m long. Its full width is also unknown but later property boundaries suggest it might have been as much as 22m wide. This would have made it a very large structure indeed, vital for unloading the stone and building materials necessary for the construction of the buildings there, and for the large supplies of food, furnishings and utensils necessary to maintain a royal retinue and thriving community. The small stone building to the west of the dock contained two large stone ovens and was perhaps a kitchen. There were also two jetties into the palace where passengers could disembark. One lay at the south end of the palace and one further north, which would have been used by the majority of people attending the palace. This was found when the tower of Big Ben was built; it consisted of a series of rectangular stone piers lying on the river bed, with pointed ends to divert the flow of the Thames and wooden planks laid over the top (Vulliamy 1849, 71). In an age when river travel was much quicker than by land, travelling to the palace by boat would have been much more popular. A gate restricted access from the river into the palace precincts if needed.

By this time the royal road, King Street, which lay where Whitehall is now and beneath the Victorian buildings along the west side of Parliament Street, was becoming lined with buildings used by courtiers and traders, inns and alehouses. The street was probably a Saxon or perhaps even earlier road and continued the route of Fleet Street and the Strand from the city to Westminster. These buildings extended across the marshy ground on the eastern side of the street which led down to the river. Previously this land had been reclaimed by drainage ditches which dried out the ground before soil was dumped to raise the ground level. A bridge must have crossed the Tyburn stream which still made Westminster an island.

RELIGION

Although there is little archaeological evidence for it, it is important to note that the city was dominated by the cathedral of St Paul's which stood where the great Renaissance cathedral of Sir Christopher Wren now stands. The old Saxon cathedral of St Paul's was rebuilt, after a fire, by Bishop Maurice, beginning in 1087. It consisted of a nave of eleven bays – probably built in the middle of the twelfth century, which can be seen in Hollar's view of 1656 – as well as transepts and a choir, which was replaced in the thirteenth century.

Parish churches

It is difficult to be certain when many of the city's parish churches were founded but it is likely that many began to appear in the late eleventh and early twelfth centuries. They proliferated to such an extent that there were eventually almost 100 within the city walls alone and 110 within the city's jurisdiction. Often these were founded by groups of individuals who wanted their own church and their own priest, which created many tiny parishes right across the city. Almost all were destroyed in the Great Fire of 1666 but the remains of some have been excavated. Four exhibit the simplicity of these buildings: St Mary Aldermanbury just to the west of the Guildhall, St Pancras and St Benet Sherehog to the south of Cheapside, and St Nicholas Shambles in the north-west corner of the city. St Mary Aldermanbury – most of which was moved to

Fig. 15. St Mary Aldermanbury looking east (photo: author)

Missouri, USA, although its foundations still survive – was slightly more elaborate in having aisles and a central nave (Fig. 15). St Pancras is first mentioned in 1038 and therefore may just predate this period, but there is no archaeological evidence for the date of the building excavated and it may have been constructed after the Norman Conquest. It consisted of a rectangular nave about 8m long and 6m wide with an apsidal chancel. The walls were built from Kentish ragstone and there was evidence to suggest that they were rendered on the inside (and most probably painted). Some areas of tiled floor survived the insertion of burials within the church.

The simplest of all was the church of St Benet Sherehog (Fig. 16), the adjacent parish to the east of St Pancras. It was a simple single-celled rectangular building constructed either just before or just after the Norman Conquest. It had limestone quoins at the corners while most of the rest of the building was constructed from reused Roman building material which must have been plentiful in the area. It consisted of Kentish ragstone interspersed with courses of tile to even up the irregular stones. The floor was a simple mortar one, and there were opposite doors on the north and south sides suggesting that it could have been entered from either Cheapside or Sise Lane. In a yard to the south of the church were timber buildings, one with extensive

Fig. 16. St Benet Sherehog looking north-west (photo: MoLAS)

hearths and fragments of crucibles which might have been used for silver-working (Rowsome 2000, 55). This illustrates how much busier the church and its churchyard were in the pre-Reformation era.

St Nicholas Shambles was also, initially, a simple church. Later destruction had removed all floor levels and the superstructure of the walls as well as the upper courses of the foundations. Indeed the site was probably truncated to about 1m below the medieval ground surface (Riviere in White 1988, 8). The foundations do, however, give a picture of the layout of the church. The earliest documentary reference to the church is 1187 and possibly 1144 (Dyson in White 1988, 8) but the archaeological evidence suggests a construction date of sometime in the eleventh century although there is no reason to suppose that the church was pre-Conquest in origin. The earliest church comprised a rectangular nave at least 20m long (the west end lay under King Edward Street to the west) and a little over 9.5m wide. To its east lay a slightly narrower chancel about 8m long. In the second half of the twelfth century, or perhaps even later, the chancel was extended by a little over 7.5m (Riviere in White 1988, 8). Associated with the church were some 234 articulated skeletons.

Because of the serious truncation from later buildings, many of the burials had been removed and it was impossible to know whether the skeletons excavated were associated with the twelfth-century church or whether some dated to later periods. It has been assumed by the excavators that the burials date to the eleventh and twelfth centuries because of their relative depth and the lack of later pottery in the cemetery soils (Schofield in White 1988, 9). This interpretation is hazardous as cemetery excavations (for example at St Mary Spital) have demonstrated that artefact residuality is extremely high and that grave depths can vary widely. The excavators do, however, accept that there may be some later burials in the assemblage but have no way of being able to tell. Of the burials themselves only thirty-six were found to be complete. Analysis was therefore hampered, but of those burials that could be sexed ninety were male and seventy-one female. Only forty-one burials were below the age of sixteen (about 17.5 per cent of those aged), which is well below the expected level for cemeteries of this date, but this is not uncommon in cemetery excavations (White 1988, 30). There was a surprising lack of pathology (signs of disease) in the skeletal remains, but a number of interesting burial practices were noted, including the not unusual practice of placing a pillow under the head of the skeleton and pebbles in the mouth. In the case of those with their head laid on a pillow, two-thirds were adult women, which was the opposite to the pattern found at Raunds in Northamptonshire (Schofield in White 1988, 20–1). It should be noted, however, that some of those skeletons had stones around the head as opposed to beneath it, which may be a different type of burial practice (Barney Sloane, pers comm).

Religious houses

As with England's other major towns, London attracted numerous religious houses, although the capital's size and wealth meant that it had a greater number of them than any other English town. The lack of foundations in the eleventh century does tend to suggest, however, that London's position in the kingdom at that time was by no means the one of dominance that it achieved by the end of the twelfth century. Indeed, London's monastic foundations were quite slow to develop.

Abbey of St Peter at Westminster

The earliest foundation in the urban core was the pre-existing Abbey of St Peter at Westminster. The rebuilding of the church had been started and mostly completed during the reign of Edward the Confessor as a specific royal

Fig. 17. The inside of the great drain at Westminster Abbey (photo: MoLAS)

church. The abbey held the coronations of two kings in 1066: Harold and William, who was crowned on Christmas Day. Both of these monarchs were clearly attempting to validate their succession by following in Edward's footsteps and being crowned there, thus setting a trend which continues to this day. Neither, however, followed Edward's policy of using Westminster as a royal burial church, and no other monarch did so until Henry III was buried there in 1272. The church would have astonished most of the inhabitants of London, being built on a scale far in excess of any other building and in a style foreign to most.

The cloister buildings at the abbey were still under construction in the later eleventh century. The surviving east range held the monks' dormitory at first-floor level over an undercroft. The refectory on the south side of the cloister was built in the 1090s and the reredorter (latrine block) added at around the same time. A vaulted drain exited the reredorter and ran south-east to deposit its contents on the foreshore to be washed away by the river. This vaulted drain still survives beneath the ground and in places is up to 1.8m high from floor to ceiling (Fig. 17). In the twelfth century the infirmary was built with its now ruined chapel of St Katherine. Here the authorities held a council which finally decided the supremacy of the Archbishop of Canterbury over the Archbishop of York. The story has it that the Archbishop of York arrived late to find the Archbishop of Canterbury already seated on the right hand of the papal legate. The Archbishop of York, not wishing to take second place on the left, promptly sat in the Archbishop of Canterbury's lap.

Excavations on the western side of the cloister found temporary wooden structures, presumably associated with the construction of the abbey, beneath the misericorde. Initially these were thought to have been buildings associated with the tenth-century abbey but their position in the archaeological sequence means that they must almost certainly date to after 1050 (Black 1976; Thomas *et al* in prep). The misericorde was a stone building adjacent to the kitchen which was used for the cooking of meat. Benedictine monks were not allowed to eat flesh except when they were in the infirmary. The huge quantities of fish bone found illustrate the importance of fish in the monastic diet (Black 1976).

The church itself seems to have undergone major rebuilding works in the twelfth century. Stonework in the western towers indicates that they were rebuilt and that the nave and original towers must have been demolished and replaced. It is probable that the facing on the nave walls is merely a later dressing of the twelfth-century nave (Tatton-Brown 1995).

Holy Trinity Priory Aldgate

The most important and earliest monastic house within the city walls was Holy Trinity Priory which lay just to the north of Aldgate, immediately inside the walls. It was founded in 1107 or 1108 by Matilda, queen of Henry I, for Augustinian canons and was an important establishment in the Augustinian order (Schofield in prep).

Predating the monastery was a cemetery documented to have been attached to the church of St Syredus, which may originally have been founded in the Late Saxon period. A total of 123 graves was found, although some of these may have dated to the priory phase (and indeed some of the burials ascribed to the priory may have been earlier). A total of eighteen graves had stone-lined cists usually using ragstone, Roman tile, sandstone, chalk and mortar. A further thirty-seven graves had their bases and/or sides lined with chalk and 7 had the sides lined with clay. There were another four buried with stones on either side of the head. These are high numbers of such burials but are typical of the period and compare well with the earliest twelfth-century burials found at Bermondsey Priory in Southwark (see below).

The south transept of Holy Trinity Priory was found along with an associated chapel and an arch which led from the south aisle of the choir into a second chapel. This arch had been encased in later brickwork and survived to a remarkable extent (Fig. 18). The foundations of the south transept consisted of a layer of large squared blocks of ragstone sealed by courses of chalk and ragstone. Another chalk foundation continuing east from the south-eastern corner of the south transept supported a standing wall some 2.5m high. The wall comprised undressed ragstone and fragments of Roman tile. A chamfered Caen stone plinth lay about 0.5m above the foundation and above this lay ashlar blocks which had been covered in plaster with traces of paint still surviving. The eastern end of the chapel was semicircular and the north wall foundation returned back to meet the south transept where there was evidence of a door jamb. This indicated that the entrance to the chapel was from the south transept and might have been 3–3.5m wide. The northern wall foundation also formed the south wall of the choir. The floor surfaces of the chapel all appear to have been mortar.

Through the south wall of the choir was an arch that led into a second chapel. The chapel foundations and the surviving arch probably date to the late fourteenth century, and are discussed below, but the original phase appears to date to the twelfth century. The majority of the facing stones had been removed, leaving the rubble core which comprised greensand, ragstone, chalk and flint. The scar of a diagonal vault rib could be seen on the north side. There were twenty-one courses

Fig. 18. A chapel at Holy Trinity Aldgate being lifted during development (photo: MoL)

of surviving greensand ashlar, including a chamfered plinth which formed the eastern jamb of the arch from the south wall of the choir into the chapel. Traces of red paint survived in places. A further seventeen surviving courses of greensand formed the western jamb of the arch which was 3.7m wide. Earlier study of the arch by John Carter in 1790 had recorded a column shaft supporting a cushion capital and a diagonal rib, but these no longer survived. The lack of weathering showed that the arch was an internal opening. About 1.7m east of the arch was a doorway running at an angle through the wall; the stones within the core of the wall at higher level indicated that this was the entrance to the base of a spiral stair in the thickness of the wall. A door which led out of the church lay further to the east. The south wall of what has been interpreted as the nave has also been found.

Priory and Hospital of St Bartholomew the Great

The area to the north-west of the city, outside Aldersgate, became an important monastic centre in the twelfth century. Three monastic establishments were

Fig. 19. The choir of St Bartholomew the Great looking east (photo: author)

founded here: the Priory and Hospital of St Bartholomew the Great in 1123, the nunnery of St Mary de fonte in 1144, to the north of where Clerkenwell Green now lies, and the Priory of St John of Jerusalem (the head house of the Knights of St John in England) also in 1144, to the south of Clerkenwell Green.

The Priory and Hospital of St Bartholomew the Great was founded by the adventurer Rahere; it lay just outside the city wall alongside Aldersgate Street and much still survives. The establishment was ultimately split between the hospital on the west side of the street of Little Britain and the Augustinian priory to the east. Little of the hospital has been excavated but the hospital church of St Bartholomew the Less still survives in part. Parts of the priory church of St Bartholomew the Great also survive. The west door which now fronts on to the street was originally the west door of the nave which was demolished at the Dissolution. The crossing, parts of the transepts and the choir date to the mid-twelfth century (Fig. 19) but the Lady Chapel is a later addition. In 1955 excavations on the south side of the church established from foundations and robbed-out walls the layout of the cloister with its alley and the refectory on the south side. Fragments of walls from the west range were uncovered as were walls to the south of the refectory which were probably part of the kitchen (Grimes 1968, 199).

Priory of St John Clerkenwell

On the other side of Smithfield, an open space used for executions and for fairs (a rather incongruous mixture), was the Priory of St John Clerkenwell. As with many of the other monastic houses of London, work on recording the below-ground and above-ground remains at St John's Priory in Clerkenwell has been carried out on and off for more than a century. More properly called the Priory of the Order of the Hospital of St John of Jerusalem, the priory was the head house of the Hospitallers in England and was founded in 1144 by Jorden de Bricet and his wife Muriel de Munteni, as was St Mary Clerkenwell (Sloane and Malcolm in prep). The Order itself had been founded initially in the late eleventh century to look after pilgrims on their way to Jerusalem, but by the middle of the twelfth century it had taken on military duties. The site of the priory lies on the east side of the River Fleet with St John Street to its west and the nunnery of St Mary Clerkenwell (see below) immediately to its north. Topographically, the site comprised a plateau of ground with land sloping away on the southern, western and eastern sides.

The church consisted of a round nave, almost 20m in diameter internally, with an aisle-less chancel over a crypt (Fig. 20). Round naves were commonly

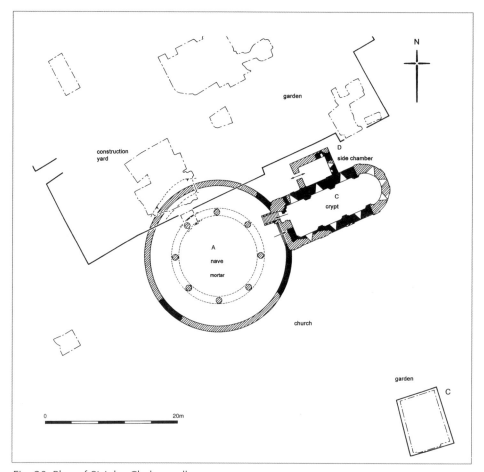

Fig. 20. Plan of St John Clerkenwell

built by the military orders in imitation of the round nave at the church of the Holy Sepulchre in Jerusalem. Three bays of the Norman crypt still survive, although the vaulting of the westernmost bay has been replaced. The outer wall of the nave was formed of a chalk and ragstone foundation, 1.25m wide, with an upstanding wall faced in greensand ashlar blocks. A circular arcade, probably of eight piers, divided the church into an outer aisle with a central circular space. The outer aisle was just over 3m wide with the inner space almost 12m in diameter. A higher level of windows at triforium level above the arcade lit the central space. The building was initially floored in mortar. At the eastern end a short flight of stairs led up to the chancel which was raised about 1.6m above the nave, and a curving flight of stairs led down to the crypt.

The chancel was at least three bays long, a little under 5m wide, and had an apsidal east end. What may have been a fragment of the altar, comprising a

Corinthian capital of white marble dedicated to St John the Baptist, was found in 1900. The chancel would have been used exclusively by the chaplains who officiated at the masses, while the knights, lay brothers and other members of the establishment would have been confined to the nave.

The crypt is thought to have had an identical plan to the chancel, which lay above it at this date. The crypt survives intact apart from some later alterations (Fig. 21). The walls were 1.2m thick and the door sill lay nearly 2m below the nave floor. Wooden steps presumably led down from the door to the floor of the crypt. The floor level was about 4m below that of the chancel and was probably originally laid in crushed chalk and mortar. The walls consisted of ragstone with Caen and greensand mouldings and there were two single-light windows in the northern and southern walls. There may have been similar windows in the eastern wall but these no longer survive as the east wall was rebuilt in the thirteenth century. Pilasters supported the diagonal ribbed vault upon which were found traces of red paint. A masonry bench ran around the inside of the walls, suggesting that the crypt may have been used as a chapter house as has

Fig. 21. St John's crypt looking east (photo: MoLAS)

been suggested for other undercrofts. An alternative possibility is that it was used as a refectory as at Strood in Kent. Shortly afterwards a rectangular chamber was built on to the north side of the chancel which cut into the crypt and acted as a semi-basement. It had a single lancet window in the east wall, and an aumbry – a small niche or cupboard in the wall – survives in each of the northern and southern walls.

A radical rebuilding of the chancel seems to have occurred by the time Heraclius, Patriarch of Jerusalem, who was in England to plead for support from Henry II, consecrated the church in 1185. Henry II attended the ceremony and on the same visit Heraclius consecrated the new Temple church. The chancel was expanded into a three-aisled structure measuring almost 22m by 16m and a fourth bay was added to the east. The central aisle was about 6m wide, the southern aisle about 5m, and the northern aisle about 4.5m. The new walls were constructed from ragstone with greensand quoins and mouldings. One respond capital illustrates the fine polychrome painting employed with a motif of palm tree crowns painted alternately in crimson vermilion and deep blue azure. Dates between the palm leaves were painted blue-black.

The northern chamber of the crypt was partly demolished and the chancel built over it. It was then used as a burial vault. The crypt itself was enlarged over the late twelfth and very early thirteenth centuries (Fig. 21). A large pit was dug and the walls set against its edges to form the expanded crypt. The crypt was extended eastwards by another two bays, slightly wider than the original bays to the west, and allowed access to both north and south. The east wall probably had a single four-light window, with an altar beneath. To the south lay another chapel with an east window, three lancet windows in the south wall and, unusually, a piscina in the west wall. The chapel did not extend all the way to the western end of the chancel, which instead was used as a burial vault. North of the central chapel lay a small room that may have formed an antechamber to a building interpreted as a treasury. This room had considerably less decoration than the other parts of the crypt.

St Mary Clerkenwell

About 1km outside the city walls and immediately to the north of the Priory of St John lay the Augustinian nunnery of St Mary Clerkenwell, or St Mary de fonte clericorum as it was more properly known. The precincts covered an area about 200m by 170m and were bounded by the River Fleet to the west and modern-day Clerkenwell Green to the south (Sloane in prep). Like many of London's monastic houses, St Mary's attracted antiquarian interest in the eighteenth and nineteenth centuries, particularly because the church was only pulled down in 1788 to be replaced by the current church of St James Clerkenwell, built by James Carr. Precinct walls were established at an early date and these almost certainly linked the nunnery with the Clerk's Well of which part of a later version survives. The supply of water was crucial to the success of a monastic house, or indeed any community, and so the well (see chapter 4) must have been one of the important governing factors in the siting of the nunnery. A gatehouse forming the main entrance into the precincts from the south dated to the late twelfth or early thirteenth century.

No archaeological evidence of the first church has been recovered, but pictorial evidence suggests it was an aisle-less cruciform structure with a nave measuring 30m by 6.4m, and probably had an internal blind arcade running along the walls. The church was laid out on a pronounced south-west to north-east alignment, apparently parallel to the southern precinct boundary. There was certainly a chapter house by 1160–2, and the founders, who were buried at the nunnery, may have been buried in it.

To the north of the church within the precincts was an early timber structure, possibly a barn. Postholes and a beam slot indicated the western and northern walls, giving the building a minimum size of 7m by 3m. About 12m further east lay a second post-built structure at least 10m long, also with an earth floor. Occupation debris on the floor contained cockle and oyster shells, fish bones, animal bones and pottery and so this building has been interpreted as a kitchen perhaps for construction workers.

Between the church and the possible barn lay another timber structure which may have been the nunnery kitchen or, if not, a domestic building. The builders had removed the overlying plough soils to create a level surface in the natural gravel before erecting their posts. The building had minimum dimensions of 8m by 5m and had an internal partition. In the middle of the southern room lay a large rectangular hearth set into the ground which was filled with mortar, rubble and burnt brickearth. Most of the other land was probably given over to cultivation, but to the east of the possible construction workers' kitchen, rubbish pits were dug to dispose of domestic refuse, presumably from their kitchen.

In the latter part of the twelfth century, probably between 1180 and 1200, the church was expanded and many new buildings were constructed in stone around it. The western part of the nave and the north transept were retained and a new choir and south transept were built. An important stimulus for these new works was the creation of the parish of Clerkenwell in 1176, and the new parish church was sited in the southern aisle. The use of nunneries as parish churches was not uncommon – St Helen's in the city served the same function (see chapter 3).

Much of our knowledge of the church comes from the pictorial records made immediately prior to its demolition. It was almost certainly arranged so that the central aisle, the northern aisle and the east end formed the conventual church, allowing the nuns access to the cloister which lay on the north side. This is typical of nunneries and often hospitals, whereas most other monastic houses had their cloisters on the sunnier southern side. The parish church was probably sited in the southern aisle, while the nuns and male members of the monastic

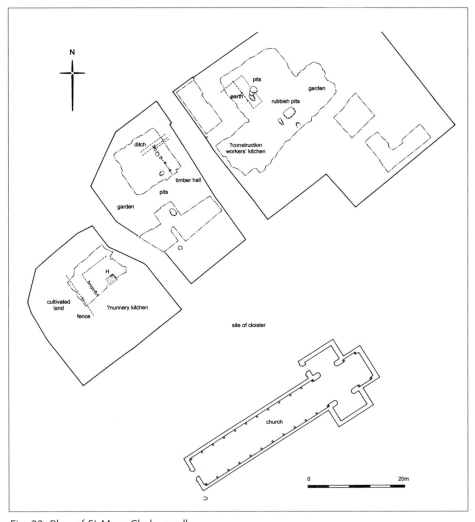

Fig. 22. Plan of St Mary Clerkenwell

community used the nave and a screen separated the two. Over the porch was a heavily buttressed tower some 6.6m square, which contained a newel stair in its south-western corner. The north transept had a large rounded arch springing from capitals supported by clustered column shafts against the wall, known as responds. It may have been used as a chapel, and a door led out into the cloister.

Many of the buildings around the cloister were built over a period from the late twelfth to the early thirteenth century. For convenience these are described here, and a plan of the layout of the monastery towards the end of the twelfth century is shown in Fig. 22.

The cloister is assumed to have been in the same location as its fifteenth-century counterpart; it measured a little under 25m by 29m. On the north side lay the refectory and on the east side of the cloister would have been the dormitory. To the north of that lay a large stone building whose west wall was found for a distance of some 26m. It was also recorded by antiquarians while parts of it were still standing. The actual length of the building was 36m and it was probably 6m wide. The antiquarian drawings show a doorway with 'zig-zag' or chevron moulding characteristic of the second half of the twelfth century, and it almost certainly belongs in the same phase of construction activity as the church, dating to 1180–1200. A partition wall divided the building into two rooms. The northern had a doorway in its north wall and a niche towards the same end.

By analogy and by its evident status in terms of its construction and decoration this building is interpreted as the guests' hall. The fine Norman doorway led east into another stone building which was almost parallel to the guests' hall. Only the east wall has been found, which was at least 20m long with a dog-leg at its northern end. The walls were constructed in a similar way to those of the guests' hall, although the foundations were much deeper, perhaps suggesting that it had an undercroft. There was also evidence of an internal partition wall and a greensand-quoined doorway. At the same time a new monastic kitchen was built immediately to the north of the refectory. It was probably built in stone and roofed in tile. To its east lay the service court, an area of about 28m by 16m laid in gravel, which was also bounded by the refectory to the south and the guests' hall to the east.

The Temple

The two major routes out of the city to the west were Fleet Street and Newgate Street. Between Fleet Street and the Thames lay the Temple, the English headquarters of the Knights Templar. Only limited archaeological works have taken place within this precinct and so the layout of their buildings is unknown. Originally the Temple was founded at the junction of Chancery Lane and Holborn in the early twelfth century and fragments of its round-naved church have been recovered. The Temple moved to its present site, south of Fleet Street, late in the twelfth century and their second, much restored church (after bombing in the Second World War) was consecrated in 1185 by Heraclius, Patriarch of Jerusalem, at the same time as St John Clerkenwell. The church consists of a round nave with a highly decorated western porch and a rectangular choir to the east. The layout and design of the Hospitaller church of St John in Clerkenwell had strong similarities with the Temple Church at this time.

St Mary Overie

South of the River Thames lay two other large and important monastic establishments. On the west side of Borough High Street near its junction with London Bridge lay the Augustinian priory of St Mary Overie (now Southwark

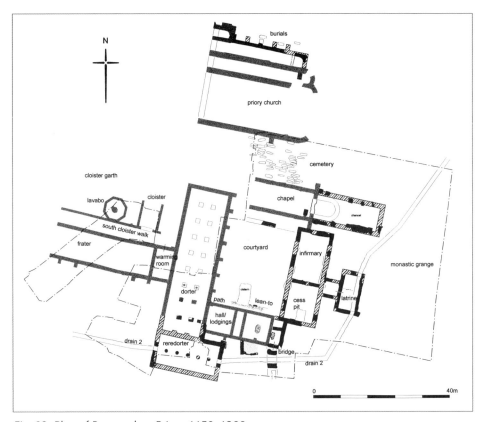

Fig. 23. Plan of Bermondsey Priory 1150–1200

Cathedral). It was founded in 1106 by William Pont d'Arch and William Dauncey with the help of the Bishop of Winchester (Schofield 1984, 48). Parts of the twelfth-century building have been recorded in the triforium gallery at the eastern end of the church and there are two doorways to the cloister and parts of transept chapels also of this date (N. Cohen, pers comm; Schofield 1984, 49). Much of the original building was destroyed by fire early in 1212. Attached to the priory was the medieval hospital of St Thomas, which was founded by 1170 and also destroyed by the fire of 1212.

Priory of St Saviour

Some distance to the east of Borough High Street lay the Cluniac priory of St Saviour which was founded in about 1089 by William Rufus on the former royal manor of Bermondsey. The establishment of the house was probably the culmination of a project originated by William the Conqueror, who, between 1067 and 1069, asked Abbot Hugh of Cluny for twelve monks to be sent to England. St Saviour's was an alien priory in England. It owed direct allegiance to the Abbot of Cluny who exercised control over the Cluniac Congregation throughout Europe. By 1100 the French Cluniac establishment of La Charité was responsible for St Saviour's Bermondsey and many other Cluniac houses in England (Steele in prep). Cluny itself, the mother house of the Order, was by far the largest and most impressive monastic house of all and survived into the nineteenth century before almost all of this extraordinary complex was demolished, so the opportunity to excavate one of these sites is of particular importance. The Cluniac monasteries in France were often sited along the pilgrimage route to Santiago de Compostela in north-west Spain, one of the most important pilgrimage sites in Christendom.

Bermondsey was sited on low-lying ground close to the Thames, and could be reached by a small river, the Neckinger. A holy Rood (crucifix) (Fig. 24) was said to have been found nearby in 1119, which attracted numerous pilgrims to the

Fig. 24. Crucifix from Bermondsey Priory (photo: MoLAS)

priory. Pilgrimage was an important source of revenue for monastic houses and such a find – whether invented or real – would have had a greatly beneficial effect on the numbers of pilgrims and the finances of the house. A pilgrim badge made of lead and tin, found near Tower Bridge in 1992, shows Christ crowned and bearded, tied by the hands to the cross and wearing a long garment. Two labels hanging down at the sides identify the shrine with a legend in black letters: (?)*signum Berm·ondsiy*, meaning 'the sign of Bermondsey'.

The church was, not surprisingly, one of the first buildings to be constructed in the early Norman period. South of the east end of the church was an apsidally ended building which was the subject of much discussion among archaeologists but is now interpreted as a chapel at the end of the church. Apsidal chapels are particularly common in the late eleventh and early twelfth centuries and comparisons with Cluny and some of the other great French Cluniac monasteries give parallels for such a building. The presbytery was an aisled building about 18m wide and 33m long. Both the north and south aisles had apsidal ends, and the north transept had two apsidally ended chapels on the eastern side. In the second half of the twelfth century a second aisle was added on the north side of the presbytery.

Outside the north wall of the church were four graves, each of which had a chalk lining with an anthropomorphic head niche. Such cist burials are common in the eleventh and twelfth centuries, particularly for high-status individuals.

Although few churches today have any surviving traces of decoration on the walls, medieval churches were brightly painted and would have doubtless been garish to our taste today. At Bermondsey stone fragments show that the mouldings and sculpture of the church were brightly painted. An arcade, perhaps the triforium, had red paint on the roll moulding and the wall face, scarlet and vermilion on the capitals, while the undersides of the arches were painted white. Figure sculpture is also a relatively rare find on monastic sites but a carved lion, naturalistic in style, was recovered from Bermondsey. Lions often symbolised Christ and others have been noted at Thetford (a Cluniac house), Old Sarum and Ely Cathedral.

Another chapel was sited in an unusual location, some 11.5m south of the church and east of the eastern claustral range, the upper floor of which was used by the monks as their dormitory. This may have been used as a chapel during the construction of the church and then continued in use as a chapel over the ensuing years. It was probably very simply and plainly decorated and consisted of an aisle-less nave about 7m wide and at least 17m long with a small apsidal chancel containing three graves. In the second half of the twelfth century the chapel apse was demolished and the chapel was extended and built with a square end, a more common type of east end for a building of this date in England.

The main cloister was on the south side of the church. The siting of the monks' dormitory with respect to the south transept of the church indicates that the otherwise square cloister must have formed an L-shape around the south-west corner of the south transept. The cloister alley was 3.5m wide; nine bone styli used for writing on wax tablets were found here, so this may have been the site of the monks' scriptorium.

The central area within the cloister, known as the cloister garth, contained the lavabo (wash-house) on its south side. These have only rarely been found on monastic sites but are almost always sited opposite the door to the refectory so that the monks could wash their hands before eating. These structures usually take the form of a simple recess in the cloister wall and independent ones accessed by a door in the cloister are fairly rare. Although the foundations had been largely robbed of their stone at a much later date, the basic form can be conjectured by comparison with other examples, particularly one at Much Wenlock. It might have been round or octagonal, with a central cistern about 2m across encircled by a trough or basin. Around the trough was a walkway about 1m wide surrounded by a wall which supported the roof.

The monks' dormitory, on the east side of the cloister, stretched from the south transept of the church down to the refectory and was situated at first-floor level. It lay over a stone-vaulted ground floor carried on two rows of piers, eight bays long. The whole building was 35m long and 11m wide. It probably extended over the reredorter or latrine ditch where it met the reredorter proper. A highly unusual room in the middle of the reredorter may have been a bath-house. This had a stone-lined drain beneath the floor attached to the inside of the building's east wall. The room was 7m long and 2m wide. Associated with it was an ancillary building, the finds from which included a copper scouring brush, suggesting that the building might have been used for cleaning utensils used in the bath-house. The latrine ditch or sewer ran under the south side of the reredorter, south of a line of three pier bases that supported the upper floor. The latrine cubicles themselves would have been installed against the south wall of the building, with chutes channelling the waste into the drain below. The drain itself was 36m long and

Fig. 25. The great drain at Bermondsey Priory (photo: MoL)

between 2.3m and 3.3m wide (Fig. 25). A timber structure comprising twenty-one posts has been interpreted as a temporary timber latrine used until about 1100 while the stone latrine was under construction.

Around the middle of the twelfth century a second reredorter was built to replace the first one. It was built further to the south and the gap was filled by an extra bay built on to the dormitory. Perhaps this suggests a rise in the number of monks attending the priory at this time. The base of the reredorter was covered with large unglazed floor tiles, which were made in the same fabric as early medieval roof tiles. These are the earliest post-Roman floor tiles so far found in London, and some of the earliest used in medieval Britain. The first floor of the reredorter was supported by a central row of five circular piers. A new stone drain was built with this new latrine block and the flow of water entered and left the reredorter via central openings in the east and west walls of the building. This remarkable piece of engineering was lined in chalk blocks with a facing and floor of ragstone. Once beyond the infirmary latrine it became a simple ditch which was found for a distance of 114m. A small bridge was built so that access could be maintained across it. The primary fill of the drain under the reredorter contained a large assemblage of pottery. One vessel was a complete kugeltopf (handled cooking pot) imported from the Rhineland, which was the only evidence for imported pottery on the site during this period. The remainder of the assemblage was common material for London at the time, comprising types such as Sandy Shelly ware and London ware.

The first reredorter was extensively altered when the new reredorter was finished. The building was extended eastwards and a hearth was laid in the middle of the west wall. Typically the hearth comprised a brickearth base with roof tiles set on edge into it. The old bath-house was probably retained and another room was provided with a central roof-tile hearth and a floor of roof tiles and stone. Such a central hearth must have disgorged its smoke through a central opening in the roof, possibly through a louvre. The old latrine was filled in and the room was also provided with a tile floor. The function of this building is uncertain but the arrangement and style of the rooms suggest a residence, perhaps for the prior. It may have consisted of a main hall with attached kitchen and storerooms. It may still have had its own bath-house and there were other rooms within the structure.

The monks' refectory, on the south side of the cloister, was over 30m long and 7.9m wide. Part of the superstructure survived, indicating that the walls had a chalk core with greensand and ragstone facing. A sculpted stone head found in the demolition rubble in the refectory may originally have come from the building. It was carved from greensand and depicted a clean-shaven youth. It was probably set into a wall and the lack of weathering showed that it had been sited indoors.

East of the cloister and between the church and the chapel lay the monks' cemetery. It was bounded on the eastern side by a ditch. It is possible that these burials continued around the east end of the church to join up with those found to the north of the church, but the relevant areas have not been excavated to prove this. The earliest burials were widely spaced in irregular north–south rows. About seventy burials were found dating to this period, with many lined with chalk blocks or plaster. Some of these had a tapering outline, like that of a coffin, and sometimes had the area of the head and shoulders defined anthropomorphically. Occasionally these structures had chalk blocks placed to either side of the head, as supports. This style of burial is thought to indicate a higher-status burial, as a lower-status burial might simply be laid in a shroud or a wooden coffin, and this may be an attempt to symbolise the structure of a church as a burial vessel (Barney Sloane, pers comm). A remarkable find was the occurrence of congenital disorders with five skeletons exhibiting the signs of spina bifida occulta. Four of these were buried close to one another to the north of the chapel, suggesting either that they were related or that the gravediggers were deliberately placing individuals with the same condition together.

Sometime between 1150 and 1200 an infirmary hall, about 25m long and 8.5m wide, was built on the land to the east of the cloister and parallel with the dormitory. It was subdivided internally by an east–west wall, indicating that the infirmary was segregated perhaps for religious and non-religious personnel. The north end was floored in chalk and mortar and the south end in gravel, where there was also a cesspit containing many animal bones, mostly of mammals. The floors were probably below the contemporary ground level and reached by a short flight of stairs. Against the east wall of the hall was a small room floored in mortar which might perhaps have been a scullery. A plan of the site towards the end of the twelfth century is shown in Fig. 23.

CONCLUSION: THE MAKING OF THE CAPITAL

The idea of a 'capital city' in early medieval England and in most parts of Europe would have been an alien one to its inhabitants. The realms of the English king stretched far and wide, deep into France including areas such as

Aquitaine and Poitou. Paris was the central city and, in those terms, the capital of France, although France was a much smaller state at the time. The principal royal palace was there, the royal burial church of St Denis lay just to the north and the coronation church of Rheims a few miles to the south-east.

As long as the English kings ruled from wherever they were, a capital city could not be defined as such. By the end of the twelfth century, however, Henry II had not only turned his palace at Westminster into a major royal residence, more substantial than his other residences, but also begun the process of making it the seat of government. Indeed, William Rufus must surely have been intending something special for the palace when he built the Great Hall there at the end of the eleventh century. This move towards London was shadowed by the Archbishop of Canterbury, Hubert Walter, who made himself a new palace at Lambeth on the opposite side of the river from Westminster, thus centralising the offices of state and religion (Brooke and Keir 1975, 363–4). Henry III finally sealed the site of government at Westminster and the rise in the importance of Parliament further strengthened Westminster's position. This meant that by the middle of the thirteenth century the political capital of England was firmly established at Westminster.

Meanwhile, a mile or so downstream, the city of London was fast out-stripping England's provincial cities in terms of both population and wealth, and its first mayor, Henry Fitz Ailwyn, was inaugurated in 1189. This gave a focus to power in London and illustrates the importance of the rise of the merchant class. Estimates of London's population at this time vary widely and are very much a 'best guess'. Recent estimates have suggested that London was inhabited by perhaps 20,000 people in 1100 and 40,000 in 1200 (Keene in Palliser 2000, 195–6). These figures alone, if correct, show the extraordinary growth of the city: a doubling of population in a century.

The period after the Norman Conquest certainly saw a dramatic expansion in the density of building and settlement area in London. However, in the late eleventh century there was still plenty of space at the eastern end of the city for the building of the Tower of London and at the west end for the other fortifications of Baynard's Castle and Montfichet's Tower. In the early twelfth century there was enough room available for Holy Trinity Priory to be built in the north-eastern quadrant of the city. This was an area which developed late, as it had done during the Roman period. Much of the basic street pattern was developed in the late eleventh and early twelfth centuries, although many of the narrow lanes which filled in the gaps probably came later. Streets such as

Thames Street were created, in that particular case to provide access behind the riverfront, making passage of goods to and from the docks easier and more efficient. Clearly much of the city was built up in the north-west corner by the early twelfth century, which may have been partly responsible for the creation of the monastic suburb to the north-west containing St Bartholomew's, St Mary Clerkenwell and St John Clerkenwell. Suburban development for housing was also under way by this time. This is clear along Goswell Road to the north-west where St Bartholomew's was set back behind the road, probably because cottages already lined the road on the west side. The same can be seen along Bishopsgate where the Priory and Hospital of St Mary Spital, founded in the thirteenth century (see chapter 3), was set back from the road at its southern end, although development here was less extensive and perhaps occurred as late as the middle of the twelfth century. The expansion in London's main suburb, Southwark, also demonstrates the rise in trade and population. Henry of Blois's decision to build a residence for himself as Bishop of Winchester illustrates the desire of important prelates to be near the capital and near the seat of political power at Westminster. Houses were built alongside the road leading out of Southwark in typical ribbon development and alternative routes were created to the east of Bermondsey Priory and to the west to St Mary Overie and the Bishop of Winchester's house.

The establishment of a quay and the breaking through of the old Roman riverside wall seem to be illustrative of London's desire to create a river frontage along the entire extent of the city. During the second half of the twelfth century the beginnings of reclamation can be seen, with individual property owners expanding into the river by building timber boxes and filling them in, thus creating more space for dwellings, warehousing and extended quaysides.

The building of houses in stone in London seems to date to the beginning of the twelfth century. No doubt many of these merely had stone foundations with timber-framed buildings above, but such foundations would have ensured longer-lasting buildings. The fashion for stone was, no doubt, encouraged by its use in the royal palace at Westminster and the great monastic houses of the twelfth century. It illustrates a greater wealth among Londoners (London has no building stone of its own and thus these materials need to be imported) and a concern for more permanency in their buildings and perhaps even greater awareness of new fashion.

That London should house large monastic establishments should come as no surprise. The military orders clearly saw the need for their headquarters to be sited in London, and the Augustinians had a group of important monasteries in London including the monastic hospitals which began to appear in the twelfth century as a direct result of the increase in population. It is significant, however, that the monasteries directly associated with London rather than Westminster should all appear after 1100, suggesting that London was not seen as an important or prestigious location before that.

The Palace of Westminster also expanded during the eleventh and twelfth centuries. The Norman rulers' desire to take over Edward the Confessor's coronation and burial church and his residence is clear and they continued to expand and develop the palace. The increasing centralisation of the state in the late twelfth century saw Westminster take hold as the premier residence and, more importantly, as the seat of government and the law.

The largest port in England by far, the city of London expanded as a trading centre. While the English kings had made a deliberate policy of siting their home and the home of government outside the city walls, they realised that it had to be nearby to be close to the heart of England's commerce. Together, the cities of London and Westminster built the foundations of London's future dominance of England both commercially and politically.

CHAPTER 3

London, 1200–1350

INTRODUCTION

By the beginning of the thirteenth century London was by far the largest city in England. It has been suggested that London had a population in the region of 40,000 in 1200 and 80–100,000 in 1300 (Keene 1984, 11–12). Its population was likely to have exceeded that of other cities in England by more than double and perhaps by as many as four times. The other towns in the local region had populations of no more than 10,000 (Galloway and Murphy 1991, 4). The expansion in its population must have been fuelled by increased migration from outside and documentary evidence suggests that, unlike many other towns where the majority of migrants came from within a 32km radius, in London they came from a 64km radius (Keene 1989, 103). It had twice as many parish churches as the next nearest city in the kingdom and it dominated its hinterland in a way that no other city in England could. London expanded through a mixture of its status as a political and a trading centre. This process, as we have already seen, was an evolutionary one. London's importance as a political centre came about during the latter part of the twelfth century. But how and why did it come to dominate both its immediate region and the country as a whole so dramatically in the thirteenth century?

LAYOUT AND DEVELOPMENT

The enormous growth in London's population led to the need for many more houses and this is clear from the street pattern shown in Fig. 26. These new streets were often alleys or smaller lanes which subdivided the pre-existing grid into smaller blocks, thereby creating new space for housing.

An example of a new street laid out in this period was found at No. 1 Poultry, at the junction of the Poultry/Cheapside road and Bucklersbury on the west side

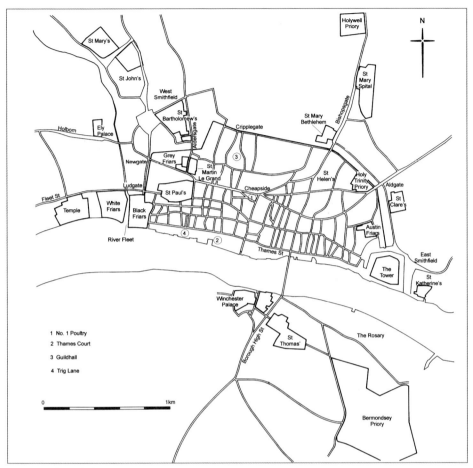

Fig. 26. Plan of the city 1200–1350

of the Walbrook stream. Here a new street, Pancras Lane, was laid out from west to east to the south of the churches of St Pancras and St Benet Sherehog. The common material for these streets and lanes in London, as it had been from the Roman period, was gravel, which is the underlying geological deposit throughout London and therefore in plentiful supply. The roads were often cambered to allow water to run off into ditches or gullies dug along the edges of the streets. These often took all manner of waste material and were consequently extremely unhygienic and must have made a dreadful smell, particularly in hot dry weather. The lack of efficient sewerage up until the nineteenth century was a major cause of disease and poor hygiene in London.

Bull Wharf Lane began in the twelfth century as a pedestrian access to the river. In the thirteenth century it developed into a well-established public lane, albeit a narrow one, about 3m wide and surfaced in rammed flint cobbles.

Suburban development beyond the city continued through the thirteenth century with areas along the major routes becoming progressively more built-up and rebuilding occurring in the core near the city's edge. On the south side of the river in Southwark, across London Bridge, work was carried out on the river defences downstream of the bridge which were in timber and similar to those along the north side of the Thames (Watson *et al* 2001). However, upstream of the bridge a series of timber piles formed the foundation to a stone river wall faced with ragstone and limestone ashlar. Interestingly this seems to be somewhat earlier than the stone river walls built to the north of the Thames in the city.

Further down the eastern side of Borough High Street, at its southern end where the road forked, a medieval well was found containing a large group of late thirteenth-century ceramics, showing the types of vessels that were in use in a Southwark household, in this case possibly an inn (Goffin 1991). These have close parallels with an assemblage containing wooden vessels found at St Mary Spital (see below) (Stephenson in Thomas *et al* 1997), and similar groups have been found in pits and wells alongside Borough High Street. This also shows that ribbon development along the street had advanced a considerable way south from the core of the settlement around London Bridge. Nine vessels were found, all jugs, made in a variety of fabrics such as locally produced London ware and Kingston ware, imported pottery from north England, probably Scarborough, and foreign imports from Saintonge and possibly Aardenburg in the Low Countries (Goffin 1991, 315–18). This illustrates not only that sizeable amounts of London's domestic wares were imported but also how important trade was to London and its inhabitants.

Development along Bishopsgate progressed with new buildings on the east side of the street. This land must have been considered as unsuitable when there was plenty of space for building, but by 1200 the eastern side of Bishopsgate was already lined with houses as far as the Priory and Hospital of St Mary Spital. Thus, when the Hospital of St Mary Bethlehem (famously known as Bedlam) was founded in 1236, it was built on the western side of the street, immediately beyond the city wall and the parish church of St Botolph Bishopsgate. To start with, the hospital probably looked after similar groups of people to St Mary Spital: the sick, the poor and migrants. It probably only started to care for the insane as a specialism in the early fifteenth century.

HOUSES

Small shops were built along the south side of St Pancras Lane, and the nearby streets of Bucklersbury and Poultry continued to be the focus of trades such as ironmongers who made bridles, spurs and knives (Rowsome 2000, 58). Behind the frontages larger stone houses were built by wealthy London citizens, often merchants whose buying power allowed them to buy up large tracts of land and build themselves more substantial and 'noble' houses.

Timber buildings were still the norm in London but stone was becoming more common for higher-status buildings. These were, no doubt, more secure, less prone to damage through fire, rotting and general wear and tear, and were a statement of wealth and social status. One such building at the junction of Watling Street, Bow Lane and Basing Lane was extended eastwards by the construction of a stone-vaulted room 4m by 2.5m. The roof was vaulted in greensand and was only 1.4m high (Schofield *et al* 1990, 52–4, 75–6). This lay within a property known as 'la Rouge Sale', a large tenement that extended as far as Bread Street to the west. Another had a stone-lined well inserted into it in the late thirteenth century illustrating the expanded use of stone for other features, that might previously have been lined in timber. Another example was the use of stone for cesspits. A group of these were also found here towards the eastern side of the site and documentary evidence indicates that these served buildings fronting Bow Lane.

At some time around the middle of the thirteenth century substantial alterations were made to the structures on the east side of Bow Lane at Well Court, which provide some of the finest examples of surviving domestic buildings found in the city. Behind the earlier building fronting Bow Lane, a new building was constructed with arched ragstone foundations and also with a cellar. The walls again were very substantial, almost 1.5m thick. There were also fragments of a stone building to the north of Well Court against the Bow Lane frontage but this was almost entirely destroyed by a later very substantial building on the same site. This too had arched ragstone foundations typical of early to mid-thirteenth-century construction, indeed very similar to those used in the infirmary at St Mary Spital dating to after 1235 (see below). This building was also cellared and fronted on to both Bow Lane and Well Court, indicating that Well Court was certainly in existence by the thirteenth century. It had a doorway opening on to Well Court in the south-east corner and there was presumably a staircase which descended into the cellar in the thickness of the wall. The earliest floors in the cellar were of clay. To the east lay a stone undercroft about 8m square with parts of the greensand vaulting still intact. The vault sprang from 1.5m above the cellar floor with its apex a further 1.6m above the springing line. There was a small niche in the west wall, about 0.4m above the floor, and a garderobe to the east of the building (Schofield *et al* 1990, 82–8).

Similar stone structures, three in total, were found at Milk Street, and a new alley was laid out, known as Robinson's Court. North of the alley were two stone buildings, the first originally a ground-floor structure and the second with a cellar. This cellar was reached from the street via a stair in the south-west corner (Schofield *et al* 1990, 124–8). Behind each of the properties was a stone-lined cesspit and two had their own wells. The cesspit associated with the south-western property contained a ceramic crucible, a glass urinal, two wooden box lids, a group of wooden bowls and fragments of linen textile.

East of the Queenhithe dock, four medieval properties illustrate the wealth of London's merchants (Ayre *et al* in prep). These presumably fronted on to the river to the south and Thames Street to the north. The properties would therefore have been at least 53m long and were about 7–8m wide. Often they reused earlier divisions dating back to the tenth and eleventh centuries. In general only the stone foundations had survived later destruction.

The western property, which bordered the dock, had as its west wall the riverside wall which was extended southwards by the construction of an undercroft. Part of the west side of Bull Wharf Lane had escaped the later truncation which characterised the rest of the site and here the eastern part of a stone undercroft was discovered which measured in total 5.6m by 4.4m. Much of the rest of the structure had been destroyed but the well-surviving section gives a good impression of the type of house in use by a middle-ranking member of society. It had two windows with splayed embrasures in the eastern wall. In between these was a door which led into an entrance hall from the lane. This hall led into undercrofts on either side and a stair to the upper floor which may have been timber-framed. The house may have extended all the way north to Thames Street. Evidence of sockets and corroded iron bars plus an additional grille over the windows indicates that the owners made strenuous efforts to prevent anyone breaking into the undercroft, presumably because it was used to store whatever wares the owner sold which were clearly considered valuable. The lack of evidence for vaulting or any central supports suggests that the undercroft was roofed in timber, a slightly less high-status structure than a stone-vaulted undercroft. This building was owned, and probably built, by a man named William de Medelane, a dyer, who died in 1313. The archaeological evidence suggests the house was built in the last quarter of the thirteenth century; it was described as having two solars in 1318.

Only foundations from the other three properties were found, with no surviving floor levels, but the buildings in the eastern property were described as tenements, shops, solars and cellars in documents of the period, and no doubt almost all of the buildings in the area would have served those basic functions.

Behind the waterfronts at Trig Lane a large area of medieval houses was uncovered (Milne and Milne 1981, 32–5). The earliest were in timber but often no trace of the wood survived and only the presence of internal mortar floor surfaces indicated that there had been structures there. In the late thirteenth century a small chalk structure, about 1.4m by 1.4m, thought to have been a storage area for keeping perishable goods, was constructed with its southern edge formed by the timber revetment. Its initial floor was in gravel and earth, laid about 1m below the external ground level.

A rather more substantial structure was then built at the same time as the waterfront was advanced into the Thames, probably in the second quarter of the fourteenth century. It was over 6m long and 5.2m wide internally and had stone foundations supporting a timber-framed building, probably of two storeys given the size of the foundations. The builders had clearly understood the unstable nature of the soft reclaimed ground under part of the building and had built substantial chalk footings, 2m deep, as supports. The building had a chalk floor and a partition wall divided it. At some time the building seems to have been destroyed by fire since a thick deposit of burnt material was found across the floor. Fires were no doubt a regular hazard in tightly packed medieval streets full of timber-framed buildings.

By the thirteenth century the commonest stones in use in London were mostly imported from the south-east: chalk for foundations and the central wall fillings, ragstone as a more durable exterior stone, and greensand which could be easily carved and worked. Only the very wealthiest of builders could afford luxuries such as Purbeck marble from the island of Purbeck in Dorset. Timber buildings would often have been thatched but in 1212 thatch was banned as a roofing material because it was such a fire hazard and in 1245 it was stipulated that tiles or shingles should be used. This edict from 1212 was perhaps related to the fire in Southwark which destroyed the Priory of St Mary Overie and the Hospital of St Thomas which lay within its precincts. Stone tiles or slates would have been expensive and were rarely used (Keilly in Egan *et al* 1998, 26). From this time onwards ceramic tiles were by far the commonest form of roof covering. Roof tiles were most commonly of the peg tile type with holes for pegs to secure each tile. Flanged and curved tiles were also used on roofs of low pitch and ridge tiles were used along the crest of the roof (Keilly in Egan *et al* 1998, 28).

Most houses were floored in mortar or beaten earth, and straw would have been laid down on top. Occasionally some buildings would have been floored in timber at ground-floor level on joists. Naturally, any upper storey would have had a timber floor. Only the highest-quality buildings could boast decorated floor tiles. A common type found throughout London is known as 'Westminster' tiles, so-called because they were first found in the Muniment Room at Westminster Abbey. These had many varieties of designs but usually formed part of a larger, more complex pattern. Four tiles often went together to form one pattern. The chapter house at Westminster Abbey has one of the finest surviving tiled floors in England. The place of manufacture of the 'Westminster' tiles is unknown but they may have been made at a tile kiln which was found at Farringdon when the Underground was dug in the middle of the nineteenth century. Unfortunately this was not archaeologically recorded so we may never know if it was the place of manufacture.

Window glass rarely survives and is most frequently found on monastic sites because of its widespread use there. The earliest occurrence of the lead window cames which held the glass in place in domestic contexts from the city comes from the late thirteenth century, suggesting that wealthier houses began to use window glass at that time (Egan *et al* 1998, 51).

Examples of the interior furnishings of medieval London houses have been found on a number of sites, most commonly in the large-scale dumped deposits thrown in behind the waterfronts during land reclamation. Furnishings include items such as curtain rings which suggest that drapes or wall hangings were held on metal rings from the late thirteenth century onwards (Egan *et al* 1998, 62–4). Fixtures and fittings include copper-alloy and iron keys and padlocks. These vary in size enormously, from large ones, presumably attached to a gate or outer door, to smaller ones, for use on lockers or smaller portable items such as chests or caskets. Such chests and caskets do not often survive archaeologically but the mounts that adorned them do. Occasionally these mounts were gilded or enamelled but most were plain copper alloy or iron. The mounts (and so perhaps the chests) do not seem to appear before the mid-thirteenth century and become commoner during the later medieval period. The chests were designed to be transportable so that the owners could carry the majority of their belongings easily. Most households are likely to have owned one (Brennan in Egan *et al* 1998, 65).

Domestic houses in London were lit in a number of ways. Hanging ceramic lamps were the most popular form in the earlier medieval period but seem to have gone out of fashion by the fourteenth century. Another common form was the candle held by an iron, lead or pewter candlestick which appears in London in the late twelfth or thirteenth century and some are highly decorated. Unusual examples include animal-form candle holders; one takes the form of a stag. One rare find from St Martin le Grand was a copper-alloy multiple lamp. Glass light holders became more popular in the fourteenth century (Egan *et al* 1998, 126–7). Stone lamps were also used; two fine examples with heraldic shields were found at St Mary Spital. Where no candle was used, a floating wick was placed in oil in the lamp which often led to their sooting. These were hung from the ceiling, usually by chains (Keys and Pearce in Egan *et al* 1998, 130).

Houses in London were clearly becoming more well furnished and decorated in the thirteenth century. Many had stone cellars and some were perhaps stone throughout. Greater attention was paid to architectural decoration, and the fixtures and fittings which adorned those houses are much more commonly found in the thirteenth and early fourteenth centuries, suggesting increased wealth for many of the occupants of London. No doubt many of these individuals were part of the new merchant class, prospering on London's status as the centre of trade and helping to form the guilds which played a major part in London's government.

DAILY LIFE

Archaeological evidence from the Poultry site gives us an insight into the diet of Londoners in the thirteenth century. The meat diet was based upon beef but there was an ever increasing use of mutton, pork, chicken and goose. Fish was very popular, with both freshwater and marine varieties from the estuary, while the ubiquitous oyster, mussel and cockle shells illustrate the reliance upon shellfish. Cereals are often found by archaeologists when they become charred. Wheat was the commonest to be found, with rye and oats also used. Vegetables included lentils, peas and horse beans, although these rarely survive well and were probably more common than appears in archaeological contexts. Fruit was also eaten and Londoners were clearly making use of easily available wild fruits such as apples, cherries, plums, blackberries and sloes (Rowsome 2000, 63).

The supply of water is also of fundamental importance to any settlement and a city the size of London needed plenty of it. One of the most spectacular discoveries in London archaeology was of the 'great conduit' beneath Cheapside (Fig. 27). This structure stood at the junction of Poultry, Bucklersbury and Cheapside and was a long rectangular building which provided water to the occupants of London. The water was brought from the River Tyburn, about 3km to the west where Oxford Street crossed it, via lead pipes. The vault of this building was still intact and the carved greensand quoins and doorway survived at the eastern end. This led to a staircase which would have exited up to the medieval street. Londoners descended into the building to collect their water

Fig. 27. The Cheapside water supply cistern (photo: MoLAS)

before climbing the stairs back to street level. Originally built in 1236–45, the structure found dated to its rebuilding of 1286 (Rowsome 2000, 61–2).

MARKETS AND CIVIC BUILDINGS

The site of the 'Cheapside Market' and the 'Stocks Market' near where the Mansion House now stands provided a focus for merchants and traders, particularly grocers and poulterers (from where the street name Poultry is derived). The chalk foundations of some of these houses have been recovered with their attendant yards, cesspits and wells (Rowsome 2000, 59).

These markets formed a vital part of London's economy. Feeding a population of perhaps as many as 80,000 inhabitants was no small task and it is clear that there were complex forms of markets which supplied Londoners with their food and fuel. By the thirteenth century London was the centre of a commercialised region with its population reliant upon a cash income (Galloway and Murphy 1991, 6). An important documentary study has demonstrated that food sales in the immediate London region seem to have taken three basic forms: sales in markets, sales to merchants by the producer and direct selling in the city (Galloway and Murphy 1991, 6).

Many local manors had gardens to supply them with their own fruit and vegetables and the larger ones would have sold their surplus at markets. Two specific areas for fruit growing lay close to the city walls: one across the Thames near the Bishop of Winchester's house in Southwark, and one across the Fleet in Holborn. Close proximity to the markets was important given the perishable nature of the goods being sold, and dairy products often came from near the metropolis (Galloway and Murphy 1991, 7–8). Fuel and timber were not perishable, of course, and thus came from further afield in the London hinterland.

Cattle were often reared and fattened at a greater distance from the city but still within the London hinterland. Some, however, were brought to London from as far afield as Lincolnshire. Smaller animals such as pigs and poultry could be reared in the city itself, with individual householders owning their own animals. Analysis of the butchered bones of cattle and sheep from the Priory and Hospital of St Mary Spital indicated that the inhabitants of the priory were not eating young animals but animals that had previously been used to provide milk and wool (Thomas *et al* 1997, 128).

Grain seems to have been transported by river. Henley was an important riverside town where grain was stored before being shipped to London. It has been calculated that as much as 250,000 acres of corn might have been needed to provide Londoners with their staple food (Galloway and Murphy 1991, 11).

By 1220 documentary evidence indicates that there was a Guildhall in the area where the current Guildhall now stands, and it seems likely that it occupied the same site (Bateman 2000, 65–81). Part of the western crypt of the later Guildhall (see chapter 4) dates to the late thirteenth century. The Guildhall then, as now, had as its primary function the administration of city government by the aldermen, and justice by the mayor and sheriffs. Many of these officers and elected officials came from dynastic families and proved a source of intense rivalries.

South of the Guildhall a large stone building with buttresses on the south wall formed part of a north–south aligned wing which documents indicate lay to the south of the east end of the Guildhall and might have contained the hall where the Common Council met. The wall had a fine Caen stone chamfered plinth course and the building's style suggests a late thirteenth-century date. Caen stone, from Normandy, was particularly popular in the eleventh and twelfth centuries but high-status builders clearly wished to use it after that time. South of the Guildhall lay a chapel which was built by 1299 and dedicated to St Mary, St Mary Magdalen and All Saints (Fig. 28). It was a simple rectangular aisle-less building about 6m wide with arched foundations of ragstone, chalk and flint. The upper parts of the wall were built in a chequerboard pattern of flint and greensand.

The area to the south of the chapel was simply the northern end of Lawrence Lane until the late thirteenth century when it was enclosed to become the Guildhall Yard, the name by which it has been known up to the present day. It was then common land but used by the city, and it was enclosed along its west side by a large chalk and ragstone wall which survived beneath the modern yard surfaces to a height of 2m. The yard surfaces were laid mostly in gravel or stone chippings and were constantly being repaired. Parts of a bone spoon and a lead spoon were found on the yard surfaces. Entry into the yard was from the south via a gatehouse, parts of which have been found. The gatehouse was certainly in existence by 1303 and the archaeological evidence suggests a date of the mid-to

Fig. 28. The Guildhall Chapel looking west (photo: MoLAS)

late thirteenth century for its construction. It had a passageway, probably beneath an arch with a room above. One side of the gatehouse may have contained a room, perhaps for a porter. It is interesting to note that the gate lay directly over one of the former entrances into the Roman amphitheatre, which shows just how ancient boundaries can be reused and can survive through into the modern landscape, in this case the road which leads into Guildhall Yard from the south. West of the wall around the yard was a series of kilns for making copper belt-buckles, presumably by the girdlers who started life as a religious fraternity attached to the church of St Lawrence Jewry. Nine melting kilns and one smelting kiln were found, containing the ceramic moulds for making the buckles, some of which were still inside.

On the east side of the yard, fronting on to Basinghall Street, was Blackwell Hall which was the main woollen cloth market in England. Large foundations of a building dating to the late thirteenth century formed part of this massive and important complex. The site was given by the city to Sir John de Baukwell (from whom the corruption Blackwell comes) in 1293; in 1396 the city bought the site back and it became the centre of the woollen cloth trade, especially once the city had forbidden the sale of woollen cloth elsewhere. Documents describe the building as being 34m long along Basinghall Street, with a central courtyard. The walls were mostly found as the rectangular ragstone piers of arched foundations, although some superstructure survived in places. This consisted of greensand chamfered ashlar and plinth courses. Fragments of painted stone indicate that the interior was decorated. The rooms found were floored in mortar.

DEFENCES

The city defences were clearly in need of repair by the thirteenth century – John Stow describes stone being removed from Jews' houses for their repair in the reign of King John, and Henry III had the walls repaired again in 1257 (Kingsford 1971, 9). The wall was broken through on the east side by the expansion of the Tower in the thirteenth century but otherwise reused its Roman predecessor which mostly required only repair. The ragstone walls had courses of red roofing tile and a number of sections can still be seen. In addition, at around this time some hollow rubble-built bastions were added to the wall for strengthening, including those to the north and west of the city; and Ludgate on the west side of the city was rebuilt in 1215 (MoLAS 2000, 222). One such bastion on this side of the city had been preserved beneath an early

Fig. 29. A reconstruction showing the thirteenth-century bastion found on the city wall

twentieth-century building and excavations in 1999 uncovered and conserved it. A reconstruction of the area shows the excavated bastion (Fig. 29). In front of the city wall lay a ditch up to 27m wide which formed the first defensive barrier. This ditch was used for the disposal of rubbish by medieval Londoners and the waterlogged fills of the ditch have preserved huge quantities of material including leather shoes, metal belt-buckles, a knife scabbard, wooden bowls, pottery jugs and bowls, and food debris such as fish bones, animal bones and shellfish.

DOCKS, BOATS AND LONDON BRIDGE

As we have already seen, London's heart was its dockside. This provided the wealth and commodities upon which London became the centre that it is today. Activity by the waterfronts, therefore, increased as London's trade grew. At Queenhithe, the original focus of London's docks, the construction of new and more substantial dockside buildings must surely be a sign of the increased wealth and status of the merchants who occupied this area.

Trig Lane Excavations

About 160m to the west of the Queenhithe dock, the extensive excavations at Trig Lane in the mid-1970s were one of the earliest detailed examinations of the medieval waterfronts in London (Milne and Milne 1982, 14–23). The areas examined were slightly closer to the modern river, which means that we have more evidence of the later medieval waterfronts than was found at Queenhithe but less of the earlier developments. Thanks to both sites, we now have a more complete picture of the development of London's medieval waterfront upstream of London Bridge. The earliest waterfront structures recovered dated to the early to mid-thirteenth century and probably comprised a free-standing structure built on the foreshore south of the waterfront, perhaps part of a jetty. The earliest revetment found dated to the late thirteenth or early fourteenth century and was discovered towards the northern edge of the excavation. This illustrates how the earlier revetments lay even further north, away from the river. It consisted of an east–west aligned baseplate retained by timber piles on the river side. To the north were extensive deposits, 3m deep, of organic material which had been dumped behind the revetments. This revetting seems to have been put in place as a deliberate act to reclaim land from the river and in the process to provide a secure and stable river frontage. Whether these revetments proved to be entirely successful might be questioned for they were entirely replaced by new structures shortly afterwards. The first of these was placed in a trench which had been used to dismantle the former jetty. It was constructed from a baseplate with squared vertical posts, up to 2m high, mortised into it. Horizontal planks were attached by nails to the posts and each post was individually shored by diagonal timbers out into the river. The baseplate was

Fig. 30.
Revetments at Trig
Lane (photo: MoL)

secured by oak and elm piles on the foreshore. The shoring timbers were also attached to a baseplate which ran parallel to the main one and squared timbers were set into this. The main revetment was also supported by three back braces some 3.4m apart and 3m long.

Subsequently, in about 1330, a new revetment was built about 3m to the south of the earlier revetment at Trig Lane, reclaiming more land from out into the river. This structure also ran east–west across the site and its eastern portion survived extremely well. It had a baseplate with vertical timbers set into it, retained by timber piles. The posts were set in pairs with each pair supported by a tie-back which was itself retained by vertical piles. The front of the revetment comprised horizontal planking which retained the earth dumped behind it. Contemporary with this structure was evidence for a stair or jetty out on to the foreshore to provide access to river traffic. Four timber piles ran south from the revetment to a line of eleven timber piles which lay parallel to the revetment. The process of reclamation at Trig Lane is shown on Fig. 49 and the complicated sequence of revetments in Fig. 30.

Boats

Trade through the docks was of course dependent upon boats to load or unload it, and fragments of such vessels are sometimes found reused in other timber structures. These give us a glimpse of the type of craft which filled the Thames. One such find, an extraordinary discovery, came from the site of much later Tudor fishponds alongside the river between London Bridge and modern-day Tower Bridge, close to the site of the Rosary (see below). Here, part of a boat had been reused as the side of one of the fishponds (Fig. 31). The boat was a thirteenth- or early fourteenth-century clinker-built galley which even had its gunwale surviving. Still visible on it were the three oar ports and cut-outs for the benches where the oarsmen sat. It would have been rowed by six men. The gunwale timber was an addition to the boat and the galley itself had clearly been repaired many times. Fragments of another boat were found lining a late thirteenth-century cesspit in Westminster. These had been reused from a type of boat known as a Cog, which, from dendrochronological dating, was broken up within seventy years of being built (Goodburn with Thomas 1997).

London Bridge

The earliest mention of houses lining London Bridge comes from 1221, although there is no archaeological evidence for this (Watson *et al* 2001). The lining of bridges with buildings in the medieval period was commonplace and they were

Fig. 31. The side of a thirteenth-century boat reused in a fishpond (photo: MoLAS)

one of the most important thoroughfares in a city. Later medieval references indicate sixty-two shops on the east side and sixty-nine on the west, and that craftsmen worked in the storeys above. The second pier from the southern end of the bridge included a gatehouse known as the 'Stonegate' which was certainly in existence by 1258. It included a portcullis and two hexagonal stone towers on either side. Spanning the seventh opening on the bridge was a drawbridge lowered from a stone gatehouse which was presumably part of the original construction but also first mentioned in 1258. The drawbridge was designed to allow larger ships to sail upstream without having to lower their masts.

PALACES

As the seat of the king, many nobles and bishops and numerous wealthy citizens, one of London's most obvious characteristics compared with other

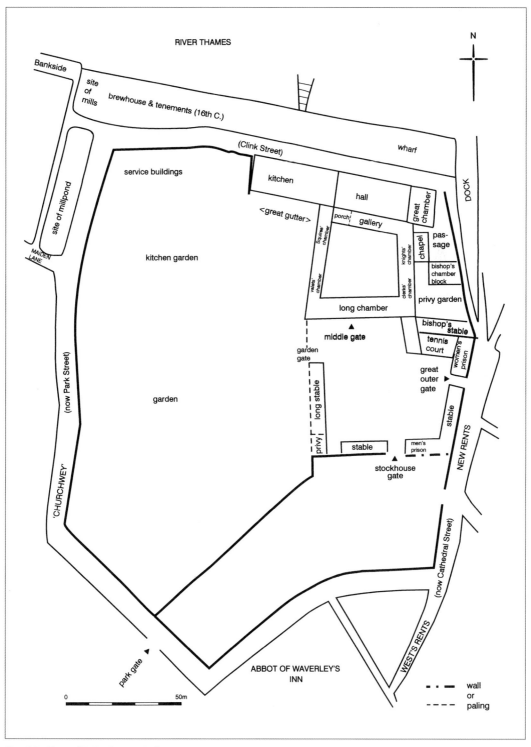

Fig. 32. Plan of Winchester Palace

English cities was the enormous number of high-status mansions and palaces that were built there. The focus for many of these was the western suburb along Fleet Street and, in particular, the Strand. This location was obviously one of great benefit to the inhabitants. The sites were by the river and they were located midway between the economic centre of the city of London and the political centre of Westminster. The Dukes of Lancaster built a mansion there, known as the Savoy, from 1270 and this was the home of John of Gaunt, son of Edward III. The Bishops of Durham, Norwich, Salisbury and Lincoln had mansions there too. On the bend in the river lay the Hospital of St Mary Rounceval. As the road became King Street (now Whitehall), the great houses continued with the house of the King of Scotland followed by the Archbishop of York's house. Unfortunately only limited archaeological work has been carried out on these properties; they remain a somewhat poorly understood part of London's medieval archaeology and one of the most important areas of research for the future. We do, however, have a few limited archaeologically excavated examples of houses of bishops and royalty to give us some indication of the lifestyle and wealth of the aristocracy.

We should not forget that one other bishop's residence partly survives today and is still used. On the opposite bank to Westminster stands the London residence of the Archbishops of Canterbury, Lambeth Palace. The only surviving buildings of this period are the chapel and crypt, the floor of which provides us with the earliest-known date for 'Westminster' floor tiles of about 1225.

Winchester Palace

Elements of three of the great bishops' houses in London have been investigated, with that of the Bishop of Winchester's house in Southwark being by far the most extensive. Large amounts of money were lavished by the Bishops of Winchester on their house during the thirteenth and fourteenth centuries and they turned it into one of the most opulent residences in London. A plan of the suggested layout of the bishop's house in the early sixteenth century can be seen in Fig. 32 (Seeley in prep). The Great Hall was being roofed in the years 1224–5, indicating that it was close to completion by that date. This is the vast structure familiar to modern visitors to Southwark. The west wall includes a rose window complete almost to roof level (Fig. 33). The hall was at first-floor level over a vaulted undercroft. The foundations were constructed in a similar fashion to the earlier buildings with birch piles overlaid by squared oak beams and covered with stone rubble. The walls were extremely thick at about 2m, no doubt to support the great weight of the structure above. The hall was 8.7m

Fig. 33. The Great Hall from Winchester Palace (photo: author)

wide and 41m long as far as the rose window. Recent archaeological work confirms antiquarian records from the early nineteenth century, indicating that the hall continued another 33m from the other side of the rose window westwards, giving an overall length of about 75m. Part of the way along was a passageway through the south wall which may have crossed the entire building, leaving another room at the extreme west end about 10m wide. This hall was a huge structure but modest compared to the Great Hall in the royal palace at Westminster, over a century older, which measured some 73m by 20.5m internally (77m by 24.5m externally). Thus the two halls were virtually identical in length but Westminster Hall was almost three times the width. Surviving fragments of the south wall indicate that it was faced in small limestone blocks, ragstone, chalk, flint and Roman tile. On the inside there was an ashlar plinth for a vault respond and the inside of part of a doorway was also discovered. The central wall in the undercroft supported a row of columns, with each bay perhaps being around 4.5m long.

In the late thirteenth century a new gable-end wall was inserted some 40m from the old east end of the hall and another wall was built parallel to this about 4.6m to the west, creating ground- and first-floor entrances to the hall. The ground-floor entrance in the south wall had a pointed arch. An upper doorway shows that the passage was of two storeys and its relationship with the rose window clearly indicated that the window postdated the doorway. The south wall was demolished to make way for the door but it is not clear whether the remainder of the west end of the hall was demolished; buttresses on the west wall, however, suggest that the gable wall was not attached to an eastern structure. The lower part of the wall was faced in ashlar, above which was a layer of knapped flint some 2.2m in height.

Shortly afterwards, perhaps in the first quarter of the fourteenth century, the buttresses appear to have been cut down and three doorways inserted into the gable wall. The central doorway was larger than the two equally sized doorways on either side. Evidence of a fourth doorway, directly to the south of the others, was also recorded. Two doors were also inserted into the wall at ground-floor level. A new gable was built and into it was constructed the rose window, 5.6m in diameter, which still survives. The weathering on the west side indicates that the window was external on that side, whereas paint recorded in the nineteenth century on the other side shows it was internal.

At this point it appears that the hall was joined to a service range to the west, only the foundations of which survived. The whole area has not been excavated but it was thought to extend for about 33m west of the hall with a width of

9.5m. It included a kitchen, a buttery and a pantry. The doorways in the west wall of the hall at both ground-floor and first-floor level linked the hall with the service range.

South of the service range was a two-storey western range which was certainly in existence by 1272–3 and was described as being 46m long by 11m wide. It housed the bishop's squires at the north end and valets at the south end. It is hypothesised that there was a gap between the service range and the north end of this range which was only located as far as the great drain. This stone drain has its earliest mention in documents in 1253–4. The drain was found in various locations over quite a considerable distance. It was found south of the Great Hall – where it was 0.75m wide running from east to west – and it was lined, floored and roofed in slabs of Purbeck marble. The projected line of the drain takes it eastwards to empty into St Mary Overie dock. A fall in level from a high point to east and west suggests that the drain may have emptied westwards as well, possibly into a channel which fed the Thames. The drain contained organic material, animal bone and molluscs, presumably waste from the kitchen.

An east range was built south of the Great Hall and was in existence by 1244–5. Only the foundations survived but these showed that the east wall returned at the south end at an unusual angle of 100 degrees rather than 90 degrees, giving the building an irregular shape. The alignment of this wall reflected the positioning of the earlier chapel, and not the Great Hall. The foundations were subsequently altered by the addition of arched foundations. At the same time the south wall was also altered and a new west wall was built. The south range, known as the 'long chamber', was documented as being built in 1319–20. Both the east and south ranges were subdivided by partition walls.

This continued construction of greater and more comfortable living quarters around open courtyards is typical of thirteenth-century and later developments in the design of wealthy establishments. Often these structures would be linked by cloister arcades, sometimes not. Almost always the highest-status rooms would be at first-floor level, with accommodation for retinue and storerooms at ground-floor level.

The precincts of the Bishop of Winchester's house were entered by a stone gate near St Mary Overie dock, first mentioned in 1244–5. The bishop had a set of stairs there into the dock. Road surfaces found to the north of the Great Hall indicate that there was a road where modern-day Clink Street now lies, which led from the bishop's stairs to his main buildings and also, presumably, to his wharf on the river.

Alterations were made to the waterfront structure at the bishop's house by the addition of oak beams into the previous beech revetment. Oak and elm posts were also inserted with planked revetting behind. Soil containing building waste and domestic refuse was dumped behind these timbers, probably around the middle of the thirteenth century (Seeley in prep).

Bishop of Ely's House

A second bishop's residence that has been subject to very limited archaeological investigation is the Bishop of Ely's house. This lay immediately to the west of the River Fleet on the north side of Holborn, the continuation of Newgate Street. The chapel, dedicated to St Etheldreda (the saint to whom Ely Cathedral is dedicated), still stands along the street now known as Ely Place. Originally a gate led to the main secular buildings which included a stone hall, kitchens and apartments. Excavations in areas behind the eighteenth-century houses along Ely Place have recovered walls of these buildings, possibly the Great Hall, which was probably built in 1286–90 (Schofield 1984, 65), and beyond it lay a large rectangular cloister bounded on the north side by the chapel. Decorated tiled pavements found adjacent to the chapel probably floored the cloister.

Archbishop of York's House

The third of the bishops' houses to have had some archaeological investigation is that of the Archbishop of York, recorded in 1939 beneath Whitehall Gardens when the Ministry of Defence buildings were constructed. The archaeological records are not of the standard of fifty years later and only limited works could be carried out, yet we do have some record of what must have been one of the most important residences in London. It was bought by Walter de Gray, Archbishop of York, in 1240–1 but very little from this early period was recovered. The site lay just to the north of Thorney Island and was bounded by King Street on its west side and the house of 'the keeper of the king's wardrobe' to the south. South of this property lay Endive Lane, the cobbled surface of which was found, flanked to both north and south by medieval stone buildings. Documentary sources indicate that a suite of rooms was built at the house for the visit of Edward I in 1295–6, and some substantial remains were found. Included among these was the stone river wall built from dressed ragstone and standing over 3m above the foundations; it ran north from Endive Lane before turning east into the river and then continuing northwards again. It was seen over a total length of more than 70m and is thought to have been built in the late thirteenth century (Thurley 1999, 2).

Edward II installed his queen and daughter in new buildings at York Place between 1303 and 1307. Excavated buildings of this date were found, including one stone structure a little over 6m wide and 17m long, divided into two aisles by stone circular columns. There was probably a double doorway at its east end with plastered walls. It is not certain what the function of this building was but it may have formed the hall of the complex given its importance during the later building campaigns. The main accommodation would have been at first-floor level. To the north-east lay what was probably the chapel, within which was an area of decorated tile floor (Thurley 1999, 3–4).

Tower of London

Three royal residences of this period have also been investigated in London, although the first was rarely used as such. The Tower of London was primarily a fortress but was still royal property and was the focus for large-scale building works at this time. The first phase of these works was carried out at the behest of Henry III. In the main they involved the construction of large parts of the inner ward surrounding the White Tower. The Wakefield Tower was built adjacent to Richard I's defences inside its own large ditch which was soon infilled, although the faced stonework at the base of the tower clearly shows that the ditch was originally intended to remain open (Parnell 1983, 113–14). A wall which revetted the edge of the ditch formed the foundation to the Bloody Tower, suggesting that that structure dates to the 1220s rather than to the mid- to late thirteenth century (Parnell 1983, 119). From about 1235 the curtain wall north of the Wakefield Tower was constructed up to a gate known as the Coldharbour gate, also built at this time, adjacent to the White Tower. The earliest version of this gate had projecting circular towers while the later version was a much larger angular structure which may even date to the early sixteenth century (Parnell 1983, 115). While the curtain wall was being constructed a wide east–west aligned ditch was dug westwards from the wall, perhaps as a temporary defensive feature.

By the end of Henry III's reign the White Tower was surrounded by a large rectangular stone-walled enclosure entered by a gate next to the Wakefield Tower on the south side of the enclosure. A further wall ran north from the Wakefield Tower to a gate which led into a smaller enclosure south of the White Tower which contained the Great Hall. In the reign of Edward I, during the late thirteenth century, a second circuit of walls at a lower level was added (Fig. 34) outside Henry III's circuit to produce a concentric fortification in the style of Edward's castles in north Wales such as Rhuddlan and Beaumaris. The castle

Fig. 34. The western curtain wall of the Tower of London (photo: author)

was entered in the south-west corner by a Barbican gate known as the Lion Tower which led to a bridge across the moat.

The Rosary

On the south bank of the Thames, east of Borough High Street and due south of the Tower of London, was a moated manor house known as the 'Rosary'. It was built as a house for Edward II in 1324–5, although Edward was murdered only a few years later in 1327 and the fate of the building immediately after that is unclear.

The northern, eastern and southern walls of the manor were built from ragstone and revetted the inside of a large moat. Within the moat was a timber structure, possibly a tank for keeping freshwater fish for food. The outer side of the moat was revetted in timber and wattle. Little of the inside of the Rosary can be reconstructed because of later truncation by nineteenth-century warehouses but chalk and ragstone walls have been noted with external yard surfaces. A porch to a building had a glazed-tile floor. The nature of the walls suggests that the enclosure contained substantial stone buildings. Indeed a fragment of ragstone wall midway along the southern wall of the enclosure indicates the presence of a gatehouse with an internal doorway. A wall on the

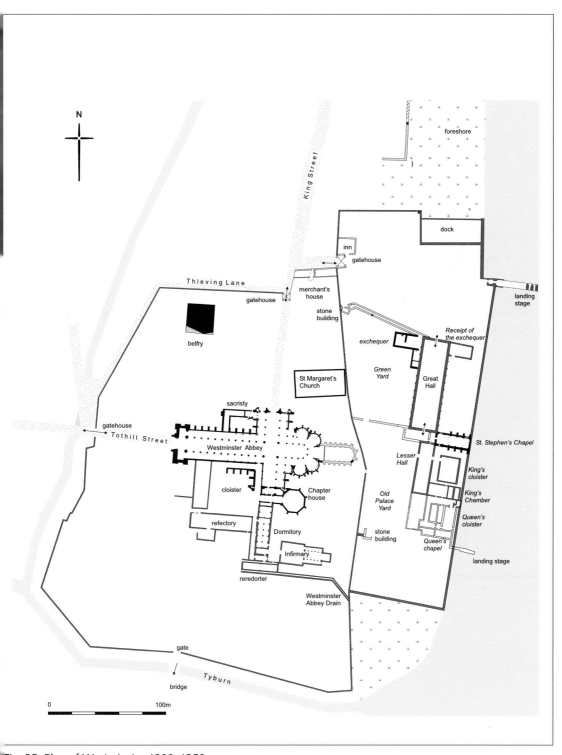

Fig. 35. Plan of Westminster 1200–1350

north side of the northern moat may have been part of a bridge abutment perhaps associated with the enormous 5m long timbers parallel to the stonework, which were possibly part of the bridge structure. Similar timbers were seen at the north-west corner of the moat, where timbers running out across the moat suggest a causeway; there was also evidence of another causeway on the eastern side. Pottery from the backfills of the moat indicate that it was infilled some time around the middle of the sixteenth century. To the east of the moat was a timber-revetted inlet from the river which was closed by a stone river wall in the fifteenth century.

Palace of Westminster

The major royal residence in London, and by the mid-thirteenth century in England, was the Palace of Westminster (Fig. 35). Indeed, from royal itineraries it is clear that Edward I was far more likely to be resident at Westminster than Henry II had been in the twelfth century (Keene 1989, 102). This increased occupation of the palace meant that there was a need for its expansion and rebuilding and for new decoration to show off the monarch's wealth and style. One of the major influences upon the layout and the design of the palace was

Fig. 36. The wall dividing New Palace Yard from the Green Yard in the Palace of Westminster (photo: MoLAS)

the formal and permanent moving of the exchequer from Winchester to Westminster (Thomas *et al* in prep). This was sited in a courtyard known as the Green Yard to the west of the Great Hall, which effectively became the centre of government with buildings for the foreign accounts added soon afterwards. The exchequer was divided into two and housed in buildings on either side of the Great Hall. The great exchequer was a rectangular stone building of two storeys which communicated with the Green Yard and with the Great Hall and the barons' meeting room, a small rectangular building divided by a partition wall into two rooms. The Green Yard was divided from the outer, public yard to the palace known as New Palace Yard by a stone wall (Fig. 36) and a gate with rooms on its west side and over it, built in 1244. This replaced a timber gate and wall, the remains of which were seen as large post-holes from which the posts had later been removed. The stone gate had a chamber on the east side, and a later illustration by Wenceslas Hollar shows a chamber above the gate passage itself. On the west side of the gate was another stone building with a dais at one end and a floor comprised of greensand stone stabs. We do not know what this building was; perhaps it was another governmental building or perhaps the 'salsary', which documents tell us lay in this yard. In either case it was a building of great importance since stone-flagged floors were rare, particularly with a dais at one end.

The public, outer court, New Palace Yard, was entered by a stone gate built in 1289. No evidence has yet been found for an earlier boundary or gate to the yard but it seems likely that there was a wall that linked the buildings next to the dock with the boundary to the abbey. On the north side of the entrance, immediately inside the gate, was a building, probably an alehouse, with a cesspit on one side which contained large groups of pottery and wooden vessels. Wooden plates and bowls were the commonest form of wares used for dining but these only survive in waterlogged conditions. The cesspit also contained barrel bases and a stirring stick. The yard itself was originally paved in gravel and stone chippings and was lined with shops and alehouses used by people attending the courts and those who had business at the palace. Timber halls, kitchens and stores were built in this yard for the large numbers attending royal coronations who could not fit into the Great Hall. No doubt the most important invitees were seated in the Great Hall, while the lesser members of society who received an invitation had to make do with the temporary halls in the yard.

The inner courtyard of the palace formed the domestic quarters of the royal household and their courtiers. Some of the finest buildings and internal decorations in medieval England were produced at this time. Under Henry III and future kings, the monarch's bedroom was painted with a series of scenes from the Old Testament, which were considered to be among the finest wall paintings in medieval Europe. He had his own personal oratory alongside his bed. A new building was erected for the queen, Eleanor, alongside the river, with her own personal chapel to the south. Another range of stone buildings probably lay to the west, all of them reached by a two-storey cloister. Most of these buildings were gutted during the fire of 1834 and were subsequently demolished to make way for Barry and Pugin's neo-Gothic palace which houses the United Kingdom parliament. Drawings made of these buildings before and after the fire give us a good indication of what they looked like. The queen's apartments, for instance, had tall graceful lancet windows which overlooked the river, as did her chapel. The king's apartments, the lesser hall and his chapel were also reached by a two-storey cloister. He too had lancet windows, this time at the end of his chamber, which gave him a view of the Thames. The new chapel of St Stephen, begun by Edward I, was a two-storey chapel with a lower chapel (still standing but heavily restored by Barry's son in the 1860s) for the courtiers and an upper chapel for the royal family. The chapel was based in conception upon the St Chapelle in Paris which was the French royal chapel but in style it was most definitely an English church. St Stephen's was fabulously decorated inside and was one of the most influential buildings on the development of Gothic architecture in England during the early fourteenth century (Wilson 1996, 192).

At this time, one of the most influential changes to English and British governance was the rise in the importance of Parliament. The king would address his barons in the lesser hall, his personal dining chamber, before retreating to his own personal chamber, the painted chamber, to leave them to their deliberations. The Commons, formed in the mid-thirteenth century at the urgings of Simon de Montfort, Henry III's French brother-in-law, usually held their deliberations in Westminster Abbey.

To the north of the palace proper, paths were laid out across the foreshore which would certainly have been in use at low tide. A large ditch may have formed the northern boundary to the royal property, although this area was rented out to others. Continuing efforts were made to drain land near the river so that it could be reclaimed for new buildings. This reclamation was piecemeal, with individual property owners reclaiming land as they required it. One owner in the thirteenth century did not wish to reclaim the land and instead built a fish-trap on it. This consisted of wattle and stake fences which were joined at either end allowing fish to swim into the trap at high tide; at low tide they would be stranded there. The properties on the west side of King Street which led to the palace and abbey had their back gardens separated by ditches which took water and waste down to the Tyburn stream.

RELIGION

Religion was a central part of everyday life in medieval Europe, and London was no different. The influence of the Church on the population was enormous and the money spent on its buildings reflected the increased wealth of the population. It was not only the wealthy members of society who endowed the church and its buildings, as Londoners of more limited means would often donate small sums to the upkeep of their parish church or a larger monastery.

The most important religious building in London was St Paul's Cathedral, which dominated the city to an even greater extent in the thirteenth and fourteenth centuries, although no archaeological evidence of this building survives. A new choir was added in two phases in 1240 and 1255, creating the longest church in England at 182m, and by 1221 the tower had been rebuilt. With its spire, this was also the highest in the country at 148m (Schofield 1984, 65).

Parish Churches

Unfortunately only scanty archaeological evidence has been recovered from the parish churches at this date in London. Nonetheless some information has been recovered. For instance, on the southern side of the Guildhall Yard stood the medieval church of St Lawrence Jewry, now completely rebuilt. However, one wall and an arch were found in a burial vault which had originally formed part of the crypt to the Lady Chapel.

Much of the lack of evidence for later parish church activity is partly because of disturbance by later buildings and partly because of the relatively small number excavated and their relatively small size which did not necessitate frequent rebuilding, extending and alteration. However, it is known that the church of St Nicholas Shambles was extended in the late thirteenth century with the addition of a north aisle to the nave and early chancel (Riviere in White 1988, 8).

Religious Houses

By far and away the largest body of archaeological evidence for London's religious buildings comes from the monastic houses which were situated throughout the area. As with so many other aspects of medieval London, the number and scale of these often dwarf those of other cities, although the relative wealth and scope of these buildings varied enormously. It seems to be the case that many of the existing monasteries suffered from a lack of enthusiasm after their initial foundation, while the new houses were much more well endowed. It was the wealthiest members of society who founded the great monastic houses, usually by the donation of both land for the actual site and land which the monastery could rent out to maintain its upkeep and pay for food and other essential commodities.

Friaries

One of the most important developments in medieval monasticism was the phenomenal rise of the Friars. These groups became enormously popular in the thirteenth century with their change in attitude from seclusion and private meditation to active preaching in the community. This meant that their houses were almost always situated at the heart of medieval settlements. South of Holy Trinity Priory, near the Tower, lay the site of the Crutched Friars, and to the west of Bishopsgate, next to Broad Street near the city wall, lay the house of the Augustinian or Austin Friars. This church survived until the Second World War with its elegant east end containing slightly old-fashioned windows of the Curvilinear style built in the mid-fourteenth century (Schofield 1984, 82, fig. 63). It was founded in 1253 and the church consisted of three aisles of nine bays (Watson 1994, 17–20). Seven of the eight columns dividing the bays on the south side of the church were found to have rectangular chalk footings, although the columns above were thought to have been rebuilt in 1354. To the north of the church lay the cloister, although the published plan reconstructed from documentary sources does not show a lane between the cloister and church, which was common in such establishments. Other archaeological investigations have recovered parts of the chalk foundations of the 'little chapter house' which was sited to the south of the 'great chapter house', and in the late nineteenth and early twentieth centuries the north range of the cloister and parts of the east and west ranges of the subsidiary cloister to the north. The buildings recovered probably represent the guesthouse, refectory, dormitory, kitchens and bakehouse.

The Carmelite Friars, or White Friars, founded their house immediately to the west of the city beyond the River Fleet in 1241, but the two greatest friaries in London were both situated on the western side within the city walls. The Franciscans, or Greyfriars, built their house just inside the walls next to Newgate, first founded in 1239. The western half of their great church, rebuilt by Wren, stands to the west of St Martin le Grand and to the north of St Paul's. Originally 90.2m long and 25.3m wide, this was one of the grandest churches in London and contained the tombs of many high-ranking members of society, including Queen Margaret, buried by the altar (Schofield 1984, 70).

In 1275 the Dominicans, or Black Friars, built their friary on the site of the demolished Baynard's Castle and Montfichet's Tower in the extreme south-west corner of the city. The city walls were extended westwards to the banks of the River Fleet to surround and protect them. Various excavations have found parts of the walls of the church and the burial ground. Reconstructed plans suggest that it had a large preaching nave with a monastic choir at the east end. To the south would have been a lane to allow the public access to the church, with the monastic cloister to its south surrounded by the usual conventual buildings of refectory, dormitory and guesthouse. To the south-east lay the infirmary cloister (Schofield 1984, fig. 54). All of these were built on a terrace cut into the natural slope towards the river.

St Helen Bishopsgate

Space in the north-eastern corner of the city still seems to have been available at the beginning of the thirteenth century as a Benedictine nunnery was built against the existing parish church of St Helen, although some buildings might have been demolished to make way for it. The nuns' choir, like that at St Mary Clerkenwell, lay on the north side of the parish church with the cloister on the north side of the nuns' choir (Schofield 1984, fig. 57). The two naves were separated by a screen. The church itself survives although the conventual buildings were progressively destroyed from the Reformation onwards. It is one of the few surviving medieval parish churches in London and includes lancet windows of the early thirteenth century in the south transept and decorated windows of the late thirteenth and early fourteenth centuries.

Priory and Hospital of St Mary Spital

Some of the most important institutions in London were the charitable hospitals looking after the sick and the poor. By the beginning of the twelfth century leper hospitals had been founded in the fields at St James and St Giles and soon after the hospital at St Bartholomew's was built. Of the many hospitals in London, two have been excavated in part. Fragments of a few buildings have been uncovered at St Thomas's in Southwark, which stood where Guy's Hospital now stands, and a large part of St Mary-without-Bishopsgate (or St Mary Spital as it became known) which lay alongside Bishopsgate, about 400m outside the city. This is the most extensively excavated medieval hospital in Britain (Thomas *et al* 1997). It was founded by London citizens in 1197, in particular Walter and Roisia Brunius, but was refounded on a grand scale in 1235 (Fig. 37). It was intended to cater for the sick poor and women in childbirth and to look after the children of women who died in childbirth, up to the age of seven.

The initial foundation was probably little more than a simple rectangular hall for the inmates (probably twelve or thirteen in number reflecting either the disciples or Christ and the disciples) with a chapel at one end. This lay alongside the newly laid road of Bishopsgate which was some 6m wide and had a gravel surface. Nothing of the original hospital and church has been found but parts of two rows of burials bounded by ditches on either side have been excavated to the south of the church.

The refounded hospital consisted of a T-shaped stone building. The church lay down the centre, splitting the north–south part of the building into two

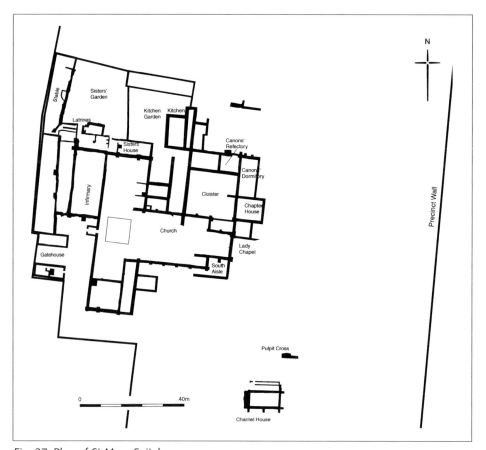

Fig. 37. Plan of St Mary Spital

infirmaries of thirty beds, one for women and one for men. The entire length of
the infirmary block was almost 60m. These infirmaries had clay and mortar
floors; the beds for the inmates were laid against the walls with a central aisle
divided by large circular columns allowing the lay sisters to walk between the
beds and tend the sick. West of the infirmary was a cemetery which contained
about a hundred individuals laid neatly in grave rows. Later destruction could
be seen to have accounted for a further seventy-five or so graves. A door led into
this cemetery from the infirmary and so clearly these burials represented people
from the infirmary but it is not clear how the hospital decided who would be
buried in this part of the cemetery and who would be buried in the main
cemetery to the south of the church. The burials west of the infirmary contained
a high proportion of adolescents and juveniles, with over half the burials being
aged under 25 at death. This has been used, in association with the small
number of dead, to suggest that a high proportion of the people using the
hospital at this time were migrants and pilgrims.

The sisters lived in their own wooden house in the Sisters' Garden. This had a
mortar floor around which were found holes where timber posts and beams had
once been. The sick may have had their own lockers, as shown by a group of
small keys discarded in the infirmary. Found in the same area was a glass linen
smoother, perhaps for the sheets which are documented as having been used to
cover the straw bedding. By the end of the thirteenth century a new two-storey
infirmary had been built to replace the original infirmary which now became a
chapel containing tombs and smaller chantry chapels with tiled floors. The
infirmary was rectangular and the upper floor was supported by a row of four
large rectangular piers. The two floors were presumably used to segregate the
sexes. A hearth in the north-east corner may, perhaps, have been used by the
sisters as a place for preparing food or warming up herbal remedies. In a pit
outside the infirmary a large group of eighteen wooden bowls and plates was
found, preserved by the waterlogged ground (Fig. 38), along with a complete
pair of leather boots and a large quantity of ceramic vessels, most of which were
jugs and of a type known as London ware. These are directly comparable with
the group found in the inn at Borough High Street (see above). The wooden
vessels had marks on the base, probably to indicate ownership, and some had
been blackened by fire. They may well have been used by the inmates of the
hospital themselves; the bowls were ideal for broths and stews, and the plates for
meat and fish. A large collection of animal and fish bones collected from the
same area indicated the importance of fish in the diet, with plaice and herring
being the most common species eaten. The fish represented had a wide

Fig. 38. A group of wooden bowls from St Mary Spital

catchment area, including both marine and freshwater species. The meat eaten was predominantly beef although mutton was becoming increasingly popular.

The infirmary was soon enlarged by the construction of a two-storey extension to cater for the increasing numbers of people coming to the hospital. A new stone cloister was built for the Augustinian canons around 1280 on the north side of the church. These buildings were recorded in the 1930s, when it was noted that both the refectory and the chapter house had decorated tiled floors. The walls of these buildings were built predominantly from ragstone with a chalk core and mouldings in greensand. The canons' dormitory was 27m long and lay on the east side of the cloister at first-floor level with the chapter house and storerooms beneath. The refectory lay on the north side of the cloister at ground-floor level and the large buttressed foundations on the north side indicate where a pulpit may have been for passages from the Bible to be read during meal times. The cloister itself was small, measuring only 12m by 10m, including the cloister alley of which no trace was found. To the north-west of the cloister, in the typical position in an Augustinian house, lay the stone kitchen, within which lay a large round oven, also built from stone.

A new water supply to the hospital in 1278 entailed the digging of a large reservoir, some 20m across and at least 42m long, to the east of the cloister, with a stone wall across it to divide the clean water from the dirty water deposited in it by a drain (Thomas and Holder 1999). This drain led from a building to the west which may have been the canons' reredorter. Further east the great drain of the hospital, which serviced the hospital latrines as well as the kitchen, exited out into Bishopsgate and was thought to have emptied into a ditch alongside the street. Excavations in 1998, however, found the drain continuing on the other side of the street across what was still priory-owned land. The drain must, therefore, have continued under the street before continuing its journey, perhaps emptying its contents into the River Walbrook.

Until the water supply was acquired, the infirmary latrines were likely to have emptied into cesspits. These were found on the north side of the late thirteenth-century infirmary, and a rectangular stone building east of the 1235 infirmary may also have been a latrine block with cesspits.

Many thousands of burials have been excavated from the cemetery, including a large group interred in pits towards the end of the thirteenth century. These pits contained skeletons up to five layers deep, and all ages and sexes were represented in them. The skeletons were generally laid out in the usual Christian way – on their back with their head at the west end – but some were found on their faces and others were buried from south to north. Well over two thousand people were interred at this time. It is not known whether all of them were inmates of the hospital or whether St Mary Spital was lending a helping hand to London as a whole during a time of epidemic disease. The vast numbers buried and the fact that they were interred in mass pits, presumably quite hurriedly, suggest some sort of major epidemic in London which required the rapid burials of large numbers of people. Perhaps each pit represented a day's worth of the dead. Currently it is not known what killed all of these people but they would seem to be at least half a century too early to be victims of the Black Death. They could have been victims of something as mundane but potentially lethal as influenza.

Elsewhere in the cemetery the usual burial of inmates, benefactors, lay sisters and brothers, and Augustinian canons took place, with each buried in their own grave. A number of priests were buried with a pewter chalice and patten: their symbolic communion set for the body and blood of Christ. The cemetery was divided from the northern part of the precinct by a large ditch about 4m wide and 2m deep. This ditch joined with another which bounded the whole eastern side of the precinct inside a large earth bank. This bank was actually created by terracing a large area on the eastern side of the precinct to flatten out the site – a colossal undertaking. A chalk wall bounded the cemetery on the west side.

Also in the cemetery a major new building was constructed: a medieval charnel house measuring about 11m by 5m internally (Fig. 39). The date of this building is uncertain but it may have been sometime between 1300 and 1350, and was built to store the bones of skeletons disturbed in the cemetery. It was half underground and was reached by a set of stairs through a doorway at the east end of the building. A staircase at the west end led up to the chapel of St Edmund the Bishop and St Mary Magdalen, which was at first-floor level. Here services were held to dedicate the bones beneath, in particular on All Souls' Day. The charnel house, found in 1999, owes its remarkable survival to its reuse after

Fig. 39. The southern elevation of the charnel house at St Mary Spital (photo: MoLAS)

the dissolution of the monastery and the fact that it was demolished down to a new raised ground level in about 1700. Its 4.5m-high walls tower above the original chalk floor of the building, with parts of the painted vaulting to the cellar still intact. When excavated much of the demolished vault was found, which allowed a close reconstruction of the vaulting ribs to be made.

The southern part of the precincts was mostly used for agricultural activity at this time. It is likely that during the thirteenth and early fourteenth centuries the hospital would have relied upon its own resources to some extent to feed its population. Here ditched enclosures suggest animal corrals and there were temporary timber structures – two rectangular and one round have been found so far – which may also have been used for keeping animals. Other areas were used for the disposal of domestic refuse in enormous rubbish pits and for quarrying the natural subsoils for brickearth and gravel.

St Mary Clerkenwell

There were continuing developments at the monastic houses in the north-western city suburb. Continued expansion of the nunnery of St Mary Clerkenwell continued throughout this period (Sloane in prep). What makes this site especially important is that the service court ranges have been quite extensively excavated, giving us a much clearer idea of the day-to-day life of the inhabitants of a medium-sized monastic house. It is clear that the authorities of the nunnery spent what little money they had in the latter part of the thirteenth century on developing this part of the precinct.

The kitchen contained a thirteenth-century ragstone cobble hearth bedded in clay, and beaten earth floors, both of which had been relaid. Over these had accumulated charcoal-rich occupation deposits containing roughly equal proportions of cooking vessels and jugs. Food prepared here included ox, sheep/goat, pig, chicken, fish, molluscs, goose and other birds; some of these had been butchered in the kitchen.

To the east of the possible guests' hall, a timber building perhaps used for industrial purposes, and measuring at least 11.5m by 7m, was built sometime in the first quarter of the thirteenth century. The finding of only two postholes suggests that it was largely constructed from ground-based sill beams with only a few earthfast posts. It may have been used for metal- or glassworking since distillation vessels and ceramic crucibles were found discarded in pits outside the building. The subsequent phases were dated to between 1230 and 1280 and suggest that the building was then used for domestic purposes. In its final phase of use there were different types of floor on the east and west sides of the building, indicating that there was a timber partition which sat on the ground surface. The eastern room was 8m long while that to the west was only 3m long. This shorter room had a mortar floor but little in the way of occupation debris and is interpreted as sleeping quarters. The eastern room, on the other hand, had a clay floor with a sequence of occupation deposits separated by patching to the floor. A layer of burnt sand, tile, slate and chalk may have acted as a hearth.

In the centre of the service yard two hearths and a bowl furnace for melting lead were found. Narrow bedding trenches from the fourteenth century suggest that plants were being grown here, and a stake-built timber structure next to the kitchen may have supported climbing plants. A fence divided this part of the yard from the remainder, suggesting it was used as a kitchen garden.

A chalk cellar in the outer court, dating to after 1270, was probably part of a two-storey tenement. The lower storey, a semi-basement about 2m deep, was entered by a set of steps in the north-west corner and it would appear that the ceiling was not vaulted, which indicates a timber floor. Another chalk cellar, this time barrel vaulted, was 2m long and possibly 4.5m wide with a maximum headroom of 2.3m. It was built on a chalk raft 0.7m thick. This is a highly unusual structure and has been interpreted as being designed for some sort of security, either for storage of money or valuables or for keeping prisoners. Both types of structure are known from other monastic houses.

East of the cloister and the guests' hall lay a large garden at least 40m square. The garden was quarried on a large scale in the very early thirteenth century and these quarries were backfilled with refuse from the buildings in the area. The refuse included very large quantities of pottery which dated to the last quarter of the twelfth century. The majority of the assemblage comprised cooking pots, and there were also pipkins, storage vessels and jugs – all likely to be material discarded from a kitchen, perhaps when a consignment of new vessels was brought in as a replacement. Domestic utensils were also prevalent in other pits suggesting that the tablewares from other buildings were cleared out at a similar time. Animal bone gives us a picture of the diet at the nunnery with half being pig, quite a high proportion; the commonest fish was herring. In about 1300 the gravel quarries were filled in and several other pits were dug to discard domestic rubbish. Cut into the garden at this level was a trench for a lead waterpipe to supply water to the nunnery. It is known from documentary sources that there was a conduit in existence by about 1190, but this pipe – dating to the first quarter of the fourteenth century – is the earliest evidence of water supply that has been excavated. Two sections of pipe were found *in situ*. The bore was 0.12m and a collar on the end of one piece demonstrates how the individual pieces were joined together. The gradient indicates that the supply came from the north, and in fact the source of the supply is known from the remarkable map of the water supply to the London Charterhouse. This shows a spring to the north near where the Angel, Islington, now stands, and it is almost certain that St Mary's used the same spring.

Priory of St John Clerkenwell

The buildings and precincts at the Hospitaller Priory of St John also developed and expanded substantially in this period (Sloane and Malcolm in prep). The Order itself underwent an array of both good and bad fortune. The loss of Acre, the last stronghold in the Holy Land, in 1291 was a huge blow and caused the Order to move its headquarters to Rhodes. They acquired the properties of the Templars after their fall in 1312, yet the Order suffered financial problems at this time. However, the Prior of St John's was admitted to the House of Lords as the premier baron in the kingdom.

During the thirteenth century the nave and crypt are likely to have been floored in 'Westminster' tiles; the nave had perhaps plain tiles with patterns of decorated tiles placed among them. At some time in the late thirteenth century the round nave of the church was demolished and replaced by a rectangular version. Initially this may have either been aisle-less or had a single southern aisle. This made the construction of a cloister in 1283–4 easier as cloisters fit uncomfortably with a round-naved church. A large stone building more than 8m long, probably the great chamber, was then constructed at the west end of the old round nave.

North of the church, a robbed-out wall, signifying a buttressed building perhaps 11m wide, was excavated. It had deep foundations and may have been part of a range of buildings forming an accommodation block. An agricultural building south-west of the church, possibly a barn, was built at a distinct angle to the other buildings of this period. It was probably aisled and measured about 12m wide and 25m long. West of the church lay a gravel yard into which were cut rubbish disposal pits containing cooking pots and a large group of animal and fish bones. The most common bones were cattle and sheep or goat which had been slaughtered when young. There were also bird bones including chicken, goose, swan, partridge and small passerines, probably skylarks. This assemblage suggests quite a high-status diet. The fish bones were both marine and freshwater varieties, including eel, haddock, thornback ray, conger, cod, plaice or flounder, sole, red gurnard, herring, smelt, cod and carp.

In the outer precinct, which may have been divided from the inner precinct by a stone wall as early as the twelfth century, early activity seems to have been confined to quarrying gravel; the pits were backfilled with refuse. This pattern is also seen at other monastic houses. One very large pit seems to have been open long enough to have held standing water before being backfilled with rubbish mostly comprising plant material suggestive of animal fodder such as hay and cereals.

The definition of the outer precinct was becoming clearer in the thirteenth century and there is possible evidence for a timber and later stone gatehouse at the southern end along the line of modern St John's Lane. There is documentary evidence of tenements being built at this time in this area, which was becoming subject to increasing development. West of the lane into the precinct lay areas interpreted as a hornworker's yard, a tiler's yard and a garden. On the west side of this lay the 'hospital croft'. The remaining land was largely undeveloped but was divided by ditches into enclosures that were used for such activities as quarrying and refuse disposal and perhaps for keeping animals. The hornworker's yard contained four barrel-lined wells and a cesspit filled with large numbers of cattle bones. Most of these bones came from the heads and analysis indicated that the cattle had been slaughtered with a pole-axe. A large number of horncores were found in the pit and it is assumed that the animals came to the hornworker from the nearby cow market from which Cowcross Street gets its name.

St Mary Overie

The priories in Southwark also underwent major changes, although at St Mary Overie this was not through choice. In 1212 the priory was very badly damaged by fire and thus needed major rebuilding. This also led to the need to rebuild the Hospital of St Thomas which was resited further down Borough High Street on the east side in its own precincts. St Mary Overie had a new choir and square-ended retro-choir built in about 1213–35, which is a fine example of the Early English style (Fig. 40). Another fire in the fifteenth century caused further damage although this was repaired. The nave is a replacement of 1889–97.

Priory of St Saviour

On the eastern side of Southwark a number of changes occurred at Bermondsey Priory during the thirteenth and early fourteenth centuries which are clear from both the archaeological and the documentary records (Steele in prep). Documents tell us that Bermondsey Priory suffered from flooding on several occasions during the thirteenth century when the Thames burst its banks, and in direct contrast to St Mary Overie it also seems to have been in serious

Fig. 40. The east end of the church and crossing tower of St Mary Overie (now Southwark Cathedral) (photo: author)

financial straits during this period. To make matters worse, when the English invaded Aquitaine in 1295, all the alien priories (that is, monasteries subject to French control) were commandeered by the Crown and put into the hands of commissioners who took the revenues and doled out modest allowances to the members of the houses.

The archaeological record shows that alterations were made to the monastic infirmary during the thirteenth century. A new building was constructed which measured about 22m long by 6.5m wide. Perhaps linking it to an existing infirmary building to the east was an east–west boundary wall which created an infirmary yard almost 20m by 10m in size. Ultimately this produced a plan of two adjacent halls with smaller structures and an infirmary yard between, as can be seen at other sites such as Castle Acre in Norfolk. Clay and mortar floors show that these buildings had utilitarian surfaces which were no doubt covered in straw. The yard wall was soon demolished and a service range built between the two infirmary halls. Food, medicinal preparations and other activities linked to the care of the sick were prepared in this building.

The chapel to the south of the church had its nave widened to the south and the building was extended with a new east end, making it 22m long by 8m wide. This new east end was soon altered. Massive foundations of ragstone indicate a tower over the east end, making the chapel altogether nearly 33m long. The even greater thickness of the foundation in the south-west corner of the structure suggests that this was perhaps the site of the staircase. The large number of 'Westminster'-type floor tiles in the demolition material within the building show that it once had a fine decorated tiled floor, while the large numbers of stone roofing tiles in the same layers suggest that they once covered the roof. This was by now a very impressive building by any standards and a documentary reference to a 'campanile' may mean that this was the priory bell tower. What makes this so interesting is that this magnificent building was not part of the main church but a separate structure. What was the purpose of this additional grand church? It has been suggested that the chapel predates the monastery and was founded by William I with the priory built around it. Other examples of these chapels can be seen on the continent, such as at Bermondsey's mother house, Cluny.

The private hall, possibly the prior's hall, became an even more elaborate structure in the thirteenth century. The building was extended 7m eastwards and a chimney was inserted, along with a new mortar floor. The construction trench for the chimney was backfilled with a huge amount of discarded twelfth-century pottery. Most of the assemblage was of a type known as Sandy Shelly ware, although other twelfth-century pottery types were also present. Interestingly, there was no South Hertfordshire Greyware, which may suggest that this was not such a common type of pottery in use south of the city. A staircase was subsequently inserted which would have led to a solar on the upper, principal, floor.

Almost a hundred further interments were made in the cemetery during this period, including one immature individual. There was evidence among the bones for fractures but on the whole the population seems to have been more aged and showed more evidence of fractures and general knocks than did those from the hospital burial ground at St Mary Spital. Such a finding seems to concur with this being the cemetery of monks living in a relatively easy, secluded atmosphere compared to London's sick poor who had to survive in much harsher conditions.

Westminster Abbey

London's greatest and wealthiest monastery, Westminster Abbey, underwent a period of massive building and expansion during the thirteenth century (Fig. 41). This was largely due to the influence of Henry III, who rebuilt the abbey as a shrine

Fig. 41. Westminster Abbey and St Margaret's Church from the north (photo: author)

to the sanctified Edward the Confessor, whose bones were placed in a beautiful tomb near the high altar. Henry also had the magnificent 'Cosmati' pavement made to surround the shrine. Henry wished to turn the church into his own personal church, his *eigenkloster*, and saw in it a way of sealing his own fame and enhancing his reputation as a king of great taste and distinction. Much of what we see today was built during his reign. He rebuilt the choir, crossing and east end of the main church and began the reconstruction of the nave, although most of this was not rebuilt until the fifteenth century. The new style was very firmly in the French mode with a chevet of radiating chapels around an apsidal east end. It would have ranked with the very greatest of churches both in scale and style.

New walls were probably built at this time around the northern precinct of the abbey under what is now Parliament Square. Within this stood the massive belfry, a two-storey bell tower about 24m square. It was founded on a chalk raft on a bed of elm piles in the silts of the River Tyburn. This extraordinary building seems to have had two corridors on either side leading into a central space, presumably where the bells were hung. It was first recorded by the famous antiquarian William Stukeley in 1754 (Stukeley 1790) and its foundations were recorded when the Middlesex Guildhall was built (Norman 1916). The precincts of the abbey were divided between the private space for use by the monks and officers of the abbey on the south side, and the public space to the north, where Parliament Square and the parish church of St Margaret now stand. The northern precinct was entered by a gate which led from King Street to the north and Tothill Street to the west. A further gate led into the southern precinct adjacent to the west gate. One of the main uses of the northern precinct of the abbey was for St Peter's Fair, which was held there throughout the month of October. By law all the other shops in London were ordered to close and thousands of people descended upon the fair to buy the wares of local traders and itinerant merchants who travelled the fairs of England throughout the year. These merchants should not all be seen as poor travellers, however. A series of stone buildings was built by the abbey great gate for some of the merchants in the late thirteenth century. One of these had plastered walls with the common style of red-painted lines imitating the outlines of the stones. A doorway, possibly with an internal arched porch, led to a path across the building to a stone set in the wall with evidence of a wooden plank on it. Perhaps this held a statue of some kind (Thomas *et al* in prep). Clearly this was a building of some status and it is documented that the three buildings on the site were let for the fabulous sum of £89 in 1289, a fortune at the time (Rosser 1989). They did not, however, warrant tiled floors and were only floored in earth, mortar and stone chippings.

A great fire in 1298 damaged or destroyed parts of the claustral buildings which were not rebuilt until the later fourteenth century (see chapter 4). In the 1930s recording at the southern end of the precinct found a long rectangular building with dressed greensand columns, which was used as the abbey granary. The building lay on the east side of a lane which led to a gate in the precinct wall. On the other side of the gate was a stone bridge which led across the mill stream to the abbey mill. The monks had canalised the Tyburn stream to create a tidal mill in the thirteenth century.

CONCLUSION: DISTINCTION AND DISASTER

London was at its height in the early years of the fourteenth century. Its wealth, created and enlarged by its docks and trade, grew to such an extent that the population was at least three times, perhaps four times or more, bigger than that of any other English city. Similar developments can be seen in other English cities but the number of wealthy houses seems to far exceed that of other English towns. Its food and fuel were supplied by a complex system of production in outlying manors and farms. These were mostly sited in the London region but some products came from much further afield. Manors owned small villages and settlements which were spread right across the region. The supplies produced were sold either directly or through intermediaries and then dispensed at markets. Goods were also imported from and exported to the continent. London dominated its hinterland to an even greater extent, with the nearest large town at Kingston upon Thames in Surrey still a relatively small settlement by comparison.

The standards of accommodation varied enormously, as did wealth. The smallest and most inexpensive properties were timber-framed with perhaps a lifetime of only thirty or forty years if they were not destroyed by fire in the meantime. A slightly higher standard of property was also timber-framed but with stone foundations, which preserved the timbers for a little longer. Many of these houses were of two or more storeys and perhaps many families might have shared them. Some had shops at ground-floor level with living areas above. The houses had simple earth floors at ground level, shutters but no glass in the windows, and may have been lit by simple candles in iron candlesticks. The inhabitants used local pottery, much of it made in Kingston during the thirteenth century, and many of the domestic vessels were of wood. Their diet would have comprised meat, fish and shellfish bought in local markets and shops, supplemented by poultry perhaps kept in their own back gardens. They would also have purchased fruit and vegetables, and lived in what was becoming an increasingly cash-based economy.

The next level of housing was the stone houses of merchants and wealthier citizens, often, but not always, situated behind the main streets on larger tracts of land. These buildings would have been multi-roomed, often with their own cesspits for their waste. They could afford more expensive ceramics and even glass vessels, and may have lit their houses with candles in ceramic or glass holders, or with floating wicks in more elaborate vessels. Their diet would have been much wider and they may have been able to afford more luxurious foods such as game-birds or swan.

The wealthiest members of society, aristocrats, bishops and royalty lived in complexes of buildings. Often these were arranged around courtyards with the main accommodation at first-floor level and storerooms beneath. Ranges were built for servants and squires. Often there was a chapel, ostentatiously decorated, and the whole complex was entered by a gatehouse. Floors were often tiled and the walls sometimes painted. The diet was even wider and more rich, although this did not necessarily aid their overall health. A wider range of glass and ceramic artefacts was used with fine wares often imported.

The docks continued to expand in London with the main characteristic of the thirteenth and fourteenth centuries being reclamation into the river. This greater desire for land must have been a result of both the increased population and the need for a more stable and secure dockside, capable of handling the large quantities of goods both imported and exported. This might also have helped to ensure that any levies or duties to be paid could be collected more easily.

The higher river levels, resulting from both the rise in sea level and the construction of London Bridge, obviously required a more hard-wearing and structurally sound dockside, and clearly London's dock builders developed newer and more elaborate techniques of woodworking and revetment construction.

Monastic houses in and around London were, not surprisingly, some of the wealthiest and most important in the country. Only Glastonbury could rival Westminster's wealth, and Holy Trinity was one of the most important Augustinian houses in England. As with other towns, London was awash with friars in the thirteenth century as a new monastic ideal swept the country. Monastic houses increased their landholdings and enhanced their buildings. Once the main church and cloisters had been constructed, new infirmary blocks were built and expanded and then the priors or abbots began to build themselves residences more appropriate to their status. The outer precincts began to be developed, often firstly for animal husbandry and for small-scale industries.

Charitable institutions flourished in the thirteenth century. New hospitals were founded at St Mary Spital, St Mary Bethlehem, St Mary Rounceval and St Katherine, to name just four. St Mary Spital was one of the largest in the country although perhaps not quite as large as St Leonard's in York and nothing like the size of the great Parisian hospital of the Hotel Dieu next to Notre Dame. At St Mary Spital we can see the type of spiritual and nursing care provided for the sick, the poor, pilgrims and migrants. The poor were still seen as being deserving of care and the Church made it clear that donations to such institutions were seen by them, and therefore by God, as being of great worth.

London and England's government also became more formalised in the thirteenth century. The establishment of the Guildhall and its attendant buildings with the newly formed post of mayor in the late twelfth century gave London a focus for its governance. English kings had always been wary of London's power and the formation of a body to govern London increased their anxiety. The guilds themselves expanded in numbers and influence from the thirteenth century onwards.

England's government became firmly established at Westminster in the thirteenth century. The siting of the exchequer there sent Winchester into decline and set Westminster on the road to a pre-eminence that it has never lost. More and more departments of state followed the exchequer: the Court of Foreign Accounts and then the law courts set up in Westminster Hall, remaining there until the end of the nineteenth century. The establishment of government and the securing of Westminster as the principal seat of the monarch went hand in hand. The formation of Parliament also occurred at this time and naturally it met wherever the king was, usually at Westminster, and thus the home of Parliament also became Westminster. The importance of both London and Westminster can be seen most clearly in the number of bishops who saw the need to own a property, often palatial, near to both.

Disaster was, however, close at hand. At the end of this period one of the biggest catastrophes ever to befall London occurred in 1348–9. This was the Black Death, bubonic plague and pneumonic plague, which is thought to have wiped out up to one-third of London's population. The plague had spread across Europe from Asia, wreaking havoc in its wake, and finally arrived in England at the port of Melcombe Regis (now Weymouth). It had certainly reached London by the end of 1348 when it was recorded at Stepney in December.

Initially the authorities in London felt they could deal with the dead by burying them in the parish cemeteries and perhaps even in the cemeteries of the monastic houses. However, the numbers of dead soon meant that drastic

Fig. 42. A mass burial trench from the Black Death burial ground at East Smithfield (photo: MoL)

measures needed to be taken and three emergency Black Death burial grounds were provided. One lay east of the Tower at East Smithfield, and two more were sited to the north-west of the city at West Smithfield: one under Charterhouse Square and one a few hundred metres to the north, subsequently called the Pardon Churchyard.

Burials from all three have been archaeologically recorded but most of our knowledge comes from the excavations at the East Smithfield cemetery. There are two separate types of burial here: individual graves and mass burial trenches (Fig. 42). It is impossible to know whether the two types of graves were in use at the same time or whether one predated the other. Perhaps the authorities thought they could deal with the dead by burying them in individual graves, but the numbers of dead made the digging of large trenches the only way of dealing with them. The longest excavated trench was about 135m long, although other trenches continued beyond the areas excavated. Their limits are, however, reasonably well defined by streets which existed at the time and the known extent of the plot. The trenches contained burials at least five deep, but it is important to note that they were laid with considerable care, with all but two laid in the usual Christian mode on their backs with their heads at the west end. This certainly contradicts the popular myth of panic burials with bodies being tossed into hastily dug pits with no ceremony, rite or care. At least thirty-eight individuals were buried in the trenches in coffins and two had coin hoards associated with them. Of those skeletons that could be aged, 70 per cent were adults and 30 per cent juveniles or infants.

Although not all of the cemetery has been excavated, and some of it has been destroyed, a total of 753 skeletons were excavated; the predicted original number in the cemetery is about 2,400. If a similar number were buried in the other two cemeteries at West Smithfield, and a similar number again were buried in the parish cemeteries, then one could arrive at a death toll of about 10,000. While this is highly speculative, the numbers are markedly at odds with the often-quoted 50,000 death figure, which seems far too high. Population estimates in London have varied from 40,000 to 100,000 (Keene 1984, 101; Keene 1989, 107). Clearly the figures of one-third of the population dying, a total population of 80,000 – or even close to that figure – and the hypothesised death count do not match: either the death count was much higher, or the population much lower, or the proportion of those dying was much lower. Archaeologists and historians have a long way to go before these numbers can be reconciled and unfortunately we will never know just how many were buried in the parish cemeteries.

CHAPTER 4

London, 1350–1540

INTRODUCTION

The effects of the Black Death were not just confined to the drastic reduction in population. Individuals were more able to escape their servitude in rural England by moving to the cities, especially London, and adopting new roles in urban life, taking over the employment and property vacated by the dead. It also led to a massive fall in the value of property which left many landowners, for instance the monastic houses, much the poorer. However, London's position as the pre-eminent port and city in the kingdom soon led to a financial recovery. While the population did not regain its pre-Black Death level until the end of the medieval period, wealth exceeded its pre-Black Death levels by the fifteenth century. Thus more money was spread among a smaller group of people, making the average wealth higher and some individuals were considerably wealthier.

The expansion of markets and the cash economy continued throughout the later fourteenth and fifteenth centuries, leading to the growth in market buildings and guild institutions and the wealth of individual traders. More land was reclaimed from the river and more permanent dockside structures were built.

The autocratic position of the Church, and in particular its wealth, led to religious tension and unease. Increased secularisation of monastic houses is clear from the archaeological record and this was obviously an important factor in their increased wealth. The Lollards and Martin Luther sent shock waves through the established Church and fuelled a desire for change in the role of the Church and the nature of religious observance. This led to the cataclysm which concludes the medieval period: the Reformation and the Dissolution of the Monasteries. However, London seems to have been a relatively stable environment for the established Church, and according to the documentary sources heretics were not widespread. The massive changes in the early sixteenth century do not seem to have been based, among the majority in London at least, upon dissatisfaction with the Church in the fifteenth century (Barron in Palliser 2000, 434–5).

Regrettably, because the later medieval deposits are closer to the modern ground surface, these are more likely to have been destroyed by modern and nineteenth-century buildings, especially in the city of London. A few important sites have survived, however, which give us clues as to the development of the city in the later medieval period.

LAYOUT AND DEVELOPMENT

The plan of London (Fig. 43), although partly conjectural, does show the increased number of alleys and lanes created in the latter part of the medieval

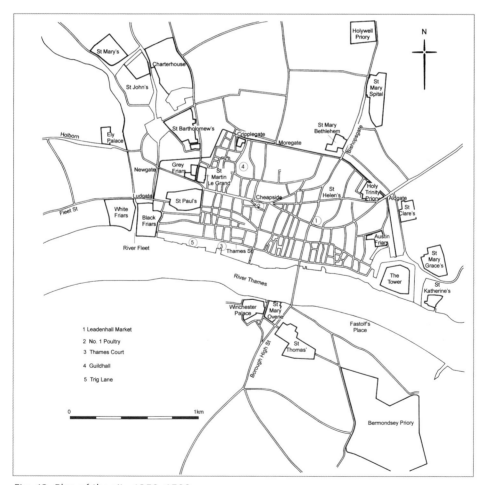

Fig. 43. Plan of the city 1350–1500

period, although perhaps the change is less than that between the late twelfth century and the early fourteenth century. The riverfront was extended further into the river to create more dock space and there was obviously a need for new housing along the grid of smaller lanes. Perhaps the fall in population made this less urgent than it had been, although documentary and occasionally archaeological evidence makes clear that large new properties were being constructed, taking over what were formerly individual tenements. New markets were built and other new establishments appeared, such as almshouses. Thus new housing must have been required for people migrating to the city.

Suburban development was less pronounced in the later medieval period owing to the fall in population and reduced need for new housing. Clearly, buildings lined the roads out of London to the north-west – Aldersgate Street and St John Street – as the Charterhouse precincts did not extend up to the road on all sides. Towards the northern end of its precincts it did have a frontage against those streets, illustrating the extent to which houses already lined the roads. The marshland to the north of the city, created by the River Walbrook, in the area of Finsbury was reclaimed in the latter part of the medieval period but, apart from Finsbury manor, there is little evidence of suburban development here. However, there was certainly increased density of building in the suburbs to the west of the city, with more inns and taverns lining the road to Westminster and four inns of court and ten inns of chancery in the district (Barron in Palliser 2000, 397).

Development in Southwark was much more extensive owing to its status as a centre in its own right. Traces of late medieval stone-cellared buildings have been found on either side of the approach road to the bridge known as the 'bridge foot'.

Downstream, to the east of London Bridge, possibly related to the rebuilding of the bridge after its partial collapse in 1437, a new stone river wall founded on elm piles was built. Again, as with the bridge, an oak sill beam supported the stonework which comprised Kentish ragstone (Watson *et al* 2001). Further downstream lay St Olave's dock which was reached via a lane from Tooley Street past St Olave's Church. The dock is thought to have originated in the thirteenth century but the earliest archaeological evidence for it dates to the late fourteenth century. The east wall was ashlar-faced and laid on sill beams under which lay a double line of piles. Much of the remaining evidence for this was sixteenth century in date but there were also three large horizontal beams thought to be part of a dockside structure. By the sixteenth century the dock was very substantial, over 32m long and about 6m wide. On the west side of the dock was part of a rectangular stone building with a cellar floored in gravel, probably dating to after 1350 when this area is thought to have been reclaimed. There was also evidence here for buildings with arched foundations dating to the fifteenth century, and one with a cellar fronted on to Tooley Street. East of the dock was another chalk cellar which was infilled in the late fifteenth or early sixteenth century.

HOUSES

Documentary evidence makes clear the increasing wealth of many of London's inhabitants. A few excavated buildings confirm this. At Milk Street, for instance, a large number of stone and brick cellars indicate the increased building activity in the area after 1400. Unfortunately the lack of dating evidence means that some of the buildings cannot be accurately dated, although it seems probable that some date to the fifteenth and early sixteenth centuries (Schofield *et al* 1990, 128–31). One of the medieval cesspits behind the Milk Street frontage, dating to about 1360–1400, contained nine fragments of woollen textile, fine glass vessel fragments and a large number of fruit stones – suggesting a fairly affluent lifestyle for the occupant (Schofield and Vince in Schofield *et al* 1990, 176, 218), and the earlier stone building on Milk Street was furnished with a large stone garderobe at the end of the fourteenth century.

Behind the river walls at Trig Lane the stone-founded, timber-framed building seems to have been rebuilt, sometime after the fire, this time with a mortar floor. Initially a chalk drain exited from the building into the Thames but this went out of use when the waterfront was extended in about 1380. By the early fifteenth century the building was demolished and a yard laid which was subsequently built over by a building which only survived fragmentarily but had a surviving wall of greensand and chalk rubble. Behind the fifteenth-century river wall were the insubstantial remains of a number of other structures including a narrow stone-built structure fronting on to Trig Lane which had a brick floor and two possible ovens (Milne and Milne 1982, 36).

The stone types used in the thirteenth and early fourteenth centuries continued in use but other building materials became more common in the later medieval period. A particularly popular style was to build walls in a chequerboard pattern using flint and often Reigate stone. This style can be seen in the London Charterhouse and at St Mary Spital. This period also saw the beginnings of the use of brick. The earliest types were small yellow Flemish bricks. By the end of the fifteenth century and in the early sixteenth century red brick was becoming more popular and this took over as the most common building material of the Tudor and Stuart periods. This preference for brick was certainly a fashion statement but no doubt its relative cheapness increased its popularity.

Roof tiles were still the normal form of roofing material and evidence of their manufacture comes from within the precincts of the nunnery of St Mary Clerkenwell. Here, a series of tile kilns may have been associated with a chalk-founded, possibly half-timbered house with a hearth which may have been a house for the tiler. The earlier of the two kilns certainly postdated 1400 but was robbed out in the mid-sixteenth century. It contained a stokehole at least 7.5m long and 5m wide. The kiln had been rebuilt in the late fifteenth century when the stokehole was blocked with burnt clay and ash from the original kiln superstructure and a new stokehole was dug. It was lined with chalk and clay. Two semicircular peg-tile flue arches were found, bonded with fired brickearth. Discarded roof tiles indicate that the tilers used a local clay and made two types of tile with varying thicknesses: peg tiles and curved roofing tiles. The kilns seem to have been abandoned between 1500 and the dissolution of the nunnery. Interestingly, tiles made in similar fabrics have been found at St Mary's from the thirteenth century, suggesting that they were making tiles there at a much earlier date, but these kilns have yet to be found. Indeed, the area seems to have been important for tile manufacture as a decorated floor-tile kiln was found about 250m south of the nunnery in the nineteenth century (Price 1870, 31–6).

DAILY LIFE

Despite the heavy truncation of many of the city's later medieval deposits there are a number of artefacts which illustrate the domestic life of Londoners from the fourteenth century onwards. While ceramic vessels were mostly used for cookery and wooden vessels for eating off, metal cookery implements were used, although mostly by wealthier households. Iron or ceramic trivets or tripods were used for supporting vessels over a fire. Copper-alloy basins and ewers for cooking and holding water were produced in England from the thirteenth century and were probably relatively expensive. The commonest types were tripod basins or ewers, although few survive well enough to give an indication of the size of the vessel (Egan *et al* 1998, 158, 161).

Cauldrons most commonly survive from the fourteenth century or later (although there are earlier examples), and are relatively common metal cooking vessels in wealthier London households. Their diameter varies from 20cm to

Fig. 44. Late fourteenth- to early fifteenth-century Coarse Border ware pot from the site of 16–17 Old Bailey

55cm. One complete example was made of copper alloy with an iron handle (Egan *et al* 1998, 170–2). Pewter flagons were typical medieval drinking vessels, although perhaps the commonest types would have been made of horn. Parts of the bases and lids of pewter flagons have been recovered and at least one complete example survives (Egan *et al* 1998, 187–90). Another fragmentary but very important material from which vessels were made in the medieval period was glass.

By the eleventh century potash glass was typical but unfortunately this type tends to survive less well owing to its manufacturing process. Lead glass, in use in Europe from the ninth century onwards, tends to survive better. Glass from the medieval period prior to the thirteenth century is rare in London and the survival of glass is generally poor compared to the likely amounts used. This is not only due to its method of manufacture but also because the glass was often reused to make new vessels (Keys in Egan *et al* 1998, 218–19).

The forms of glass types varied widely. Most flasks or bottles had wide bases and long narrow necks with no handles and were probably used to hold wine (Keys in Egan *et al* 1998, 226). Glass jugs were rare but examples of the late thirteenth and fourteenth centuries have been found. Glass drinking vessels are somewhat more common and consist of beakers or glasses more similar to wineglasses. Thirteenth- and early fourteenth-century examples exist but the commonest date for these is the later fourteenth and fifteenth centuries. Most vessels found are in soda glass rather than potash glass and are often green, although some are colourless (Keys in Egan *et al* 1998, 228–33). A late medieval phenomenon in London seems to be the use of high-quality opaque glass, similar to that used by Venetian and Florentine glassmakers in the later sixteenth century (Egan 1998, 234). One other category of important glass vessels was the urinal. These were used for uroscopy, the examination of the patient's urine, an important element of medieval medicinal practice. These vessels usually had a wide neck with a broad rim and a wide rounded base which meant that they would not have stood upright on their own.

Often the range of finds from the dumps behind the waterfronts is greater than elsewhere as not only is the soil derived from domestic refuse but also the waterlogged ground helps to preserve many of the organic artefacts which would otherwise not survive. One category of finds which illustrates something of the daily lives of Londoners is that associated with recreational activities. Music was undoubtedly an important part of life, just as it is today. Jews' harps, placed in the mouth and 'twanged' with the fingers, have been found in fourteenth-century contexts, and similarly dated or later bone tuning pegs might have been used on lyres, lutes, harps and fiddles. Bone pipes, whistles and flutes, dating to the thirteenth century and later, illustrate further the range of medieval musical instruments found in London (Wardle in Egan *et al* 1998, 283–8). Other recreational finds include gaming pieces such as bone dice and even chess pieces. The latter are made of bone and antler, and pieces recovered include kings, bishops, pawns and a rook (Egan *et al* 1998, 291–4). Other finds represent more athletic outdoor activities, including bone skates, perhaps used on the Thames when it froze over (Egan *et al* 1998, 294–5).

MARKETS

The increase in trade and prosperity, combined with an increased reliance upon a cash economy, led to the burgeoning of London's markets. One important addition was Leadenhall Market which lies in the heart of the city over the former Roman forum and basilica. It lay immediately to the east of the main north–south route through the city from London Bridge to Bishopsgate. The earliest mention of Leadenhall in documentary sources occurs in 1296, although it is clear that the 'lead hall' to which the name refers had already existed since

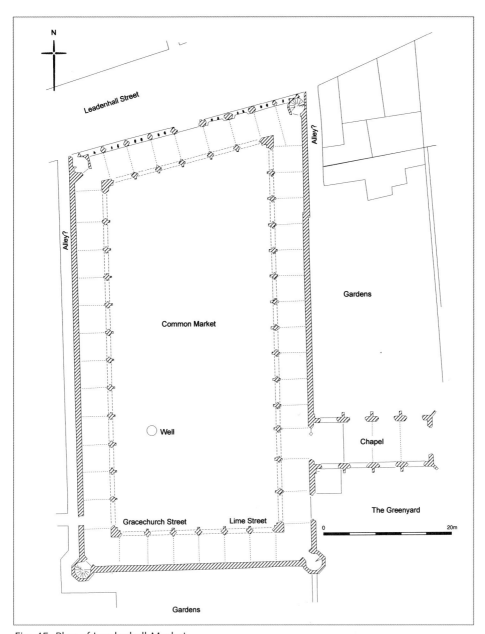

Fig. 45. Plan of Leadenhall Market

at least the early thirteenth century as part of a large residence owned by the Neville family. In 1439 the Corporation of London decided to build a garnary or garner on the site which consisted of four stone ranges around a central courtyard (Fig. 45). The foundations of three of the ranges survived, as did a section of one surviving to 11m in height. The building was completed in 1455 and fronted on to Leadenhall Street to the north. It was an irregular rectangle with the north range measuring 38.28m from east to west, the west range a little over 64m long and the east range slightly over 73m long. Projecting on the east side was a chapel. Beneath the western half of this lay a crypt, shown on a plan of 1794, which indicates that the eastern range of the garner also had vaults. Much of the building had been destroyed by later foundations and only parts of the area were excavated (Samuel 1989). However, enough was recorded, in conjunction with later maps and illustrations and particularly a plan of 1794, to gain a reasonable impression of this remarkable building.

The foundations consist principally of chalk and mortar poured in layers into a trench about 2m deep with regular rectangular interspersed sections a further 3.4m deep. This had the effect of creating foundation arches similar to those seen on many other London sites – for example at St Mary Spital (Thomas *et al* 1997, 97–8) and the Merchant Taylors' Hall (Schofield 1984, fig. 78). This enabled the builders to provide footings founded on solid ground rather than on Roman or medieval layers, without having to use vast quantities of stone throughout. The arcaded ground floor of the building was a common market, just as the earlier buildings on the site had been, selling poultry, victuals, grain, eggs, butter and cheese. This market was covered but open to the central square and would have been used by a significant proportion of London's population for the purchase of many of their foodstuffs. The first and second floors were used for the storage of grain, presumably to keep it dry and reduce the risk of infestation. A spiral staircase stood at each corner to allow the sacks of grain to be carried up and down from the granaries. Windows gave ventilation but shutters were employed to keep out the worst of the weather as the windows were unglazed.

The recovery of 177 moulded stones from the demolished building and the discovery of a well-preserved section of the western range allowed reconstructions of parts of the buildings (Fig. 46). The section of well-preserved wall lay on the west side but the moulded stones were all recovered from the north side and it is this range that has been reconstructed. The western wall on its external face had a plinth 1.54m high, surmounted by a ragstone chamfered moulding. The wall then continued for another 9.35m in height to the top of the surviving wall. The internal side of the wall was faced in Reigate stone on the two upper floors. There was also evidence, confirmed by engravings of corbels, for a timber hammerbeam roof. The wall was originally surmounted by a crenellated parapet.

The reconstructed elevation of the north range was based upon moulded stones which were recovered from the piers, plinths, windows, arches and various other components, and upon sketches and plans of the structure prior to

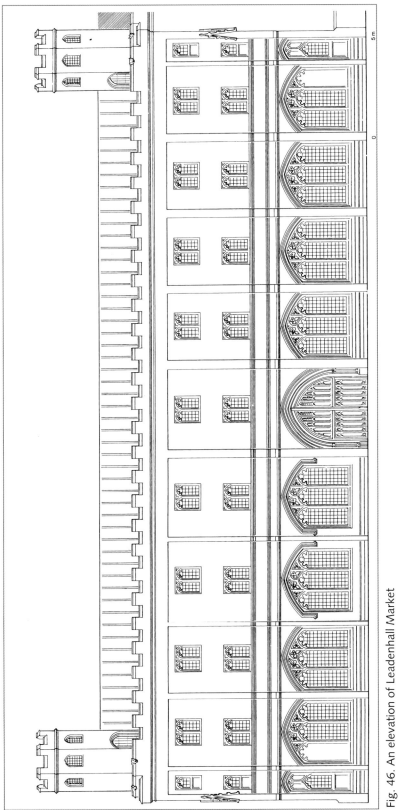

Fig. 46. An elevation of Leadenhall Market

its demolition. The types of stone used for the mouldings included Reigate stone and Caen stone.

One other important new market was that created by Edward III in Westminster. Edward set up a series of 'woolstaples' to control the taxation of wool throughout England. The Westminster woolstaple was short-lived and was soon replaced by one in Calais. It was sited in the old north part of the royal palace and was separated from the rest of the public court by a stone wall in 1355 (Fig. 50). A yard contained the market, surrounded by timber-framed houses. One of these had a back yard with a chalk well in it and a ditch behind the back wall forming the edge of the property and presumably taking waste down into the river. There was a mayor of the woolstaple who had his own house and there was a weigh-house for weighing the quantities of wool. The woolstaple was furnished with its own jetty so that wool could be brought in to Westminster, weighed and sent out again by river.

The expansion of civic and corporate buildings in London saw the construction of some forty company halls, and the rebuilding of the Guildhall between 1411 and 1430 by John Croxton (Fig. 47). The building still stands today although it was damaged during the Great Fire of 1666 and in the Second

Fig. 47. The Guildhall and its yard (photo: author)

World War (Bateman 2000, 67–74). The hall is rectangular, with high walls and a roof which has been replaced. The hall was raised above the contemporary ground level with a large porch against the south wall. Beneath it lay vaulted crypts which were partially built below ground level. Part of the western crypt dates to the late thirteenth century and was incorporated into the new Guildhall and extended eastwards. The porch still survives but its façade was rebuilt after a fire in 1785. A group of sixteen stones from the original façade was found during the excavations of the porch, reused in a much later foundation. These include part of a fine statue niche and a column capital. The niches had canopies and contained statues to the four Virtues and biblical characters.

The Guildhall chapel was rebuilt in the fifteenth century when a new western wall was built further west, lengthening the chapel. Aisles about 2m wide were added on the northern and southern sides, with a roofline lower than that of the nave. The chapel was dedicated in 1444 but work was still being carried out on the building, presumably on the internal fixtures and fittings, more than ten years later, in 1455. Often a church or chapel would have its formal dedication once the main structure had been completed but before it had been decorated and furnished. The nave and aisles were separated by arcades comprising four arches supported by Purbeck marble bases. Associated with the chapel was the Society of Pui which comprised wealthy merchants from the city. A chantry college of four priests and a chaplain was founded at the Guildhall chapel in 1356.

The medieval Guildhall Yard remained in use as such throughout this period, with its surfaces still laid in gravel and stone chippings. There appears to have been a deliberate effort to raise the ground level, so that by the time the new Guildhall was built in the early fifteenth century the yard had been raised by 2m. This raising of the ground level was probably the reason for the construction of a new gatehouse at a higher level during the same period.

DEFENCES

In 1477 Mayor Ralph Jocelin began the repair of the city wall. The postern gate at Moorgate was enlarged to form a proper gate, and Cripplegate was also rebuilt in 1491. Large sections of the wall were rebuilt in brick. The parapet was built in brick in a diaper pattern (Fig. 48) and brick arches were built behind the wall in at least three sections, perhaps as a defence against cannon (Schofield 1984, 129). This is probably the earliest large-scale use of brick in London and might be seen as the beginning of the rise in fashion for brick buildings, which were to predominate in the sixteenth century and later.

Fig. 48. The city wall, rebuilt in the fifteenth century (photo: author)

DOCKS, BOATS AND LONDON BRIDGE

Trig Lane Excavations

Some evidence has also been recovered from London's waterfronts at this period, in particular at Trig Lane (Milne and Milne 1982, 25–40). Here, at some time around the middle of the fourteenth century, a stone river wall was built. A short length forming the south-eastern corner was excavated and it consisted of a foundation of chalk rubble and timber planks while the main wall was built of ragstone and survived to a height of 2.83m. The wall face on the southern river side had a 10-degree batter while that to the east was vertical. River deposits had accumulated against the wall, indicating that the river had washed up against it.

Postdating the disuse of the previous timber revetments (see chapter 3) was a new east–west aligned revetment which was found for a distance of 17.50m. The base was formed by six baseplates joined together, into which forty-five vertical timbers, about 1.4m high, had been inserted. These vertical timbers stood side by side forming a solid stave wall in a style similar to that at the waterfront to Winchester Palace. The structure was supported by five back braces up to 2.6m long, which were held in place by timber piles. At the western end there was a return to the north showing that this reclamation was done on a piecemeal basis with individuals extending their own properties into the river, in this case by about 3m. Marks on the timbers have been suggested as representing assembly marks denoting the sequences of construction of a prefabricated structure. The sequence of reclamation is shown in Fig. 49.

Between the end of the fourteenth century and the middle of the fifteenth century (*c.* 1380–1440), the revetments were extended southwards at the eastern edge of the excavation by about 6m, showing that another owner had extended his property. This also comprised vertical timbers which formed a solid wall to the river. Behind it was dumped a mass of rubbish to level up the ground. The structure was constructed in a similar fashion to the earlier versions using back braces and baseplates retained by piles. In the south-west corner of this structure were the remains of a timber platform some 3.4m wide which was part of the original structure. It appeared to have supported some form of tank which no longer survived.

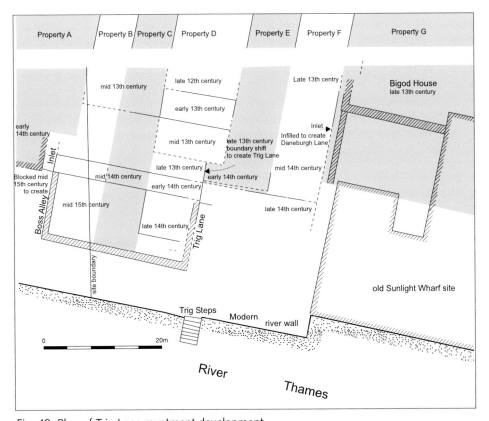

Fig. 49. Plan of Trig Lane revetment development

Subsequently the earlier timber wall was modified. A second stage was added, or more probably replaced an earlier second stage. This later second stage comprised a plate laid on to the earlier timber wall into which more vertical timbers were set, braced by six tie-backs. The eastern and western parts of this structure were built in slightly different fashions, suggesting that they may have been built separately by different owners. Interestingly, the point at which the two met was an earlier late thirteenth-century property boundary, perhaps indicating that this had continued into the fifteenth century. The reason for this re-erection of a second stage of timber seems to have been because the revetment was slumping southwards with the weight of material behind, so the upper stage was replaced and extra shoring added to stabilise the structure.

In front of these revetments was evidence for further timber foreshore structures replacing those found, dating from the early fourteenth century. Four timbers had peg holes in their tops indicating that other, horizontal, timbers had once been attached to them. Further south were three vertical posts and to the south of those a platform of planks laid over timber piles. These disparate groups progressed southwards from the riverfront and have been interpreted as the foundations for a timber stair and a jetty jutting out into the river to give access to boats. They demonstrate the vital importance to London and its inhabitants of access to river traffic and presumably these stairs were reached from Trig Lane itself, a communal access point to the river.

At some time around the middle of the fifteenth century a massive new stone river wall was constructed. It ran for 24m along the Thames frontage and then returned to the north for a distance of a further 10.5m. It survived to its full height of 2.5m and was 1m wide at the top. It was built on a raft of timbers held in place by elm piles over 0.5m long. The outer face of the wall, towards the river, was faced in dressed ragstone, as was the upper part of the landward face. Offset steps below this point were faced in chalk, indicating that they were below medieval ground-surface level as chalk would not have survived weathering had it been exposed, thus telling us the contemporary ground level. Large amounts of soil and waste were dumped in behind the wall up to the level of the base of the ragstone facing.

Boats

Since trade was so vital to London's growth and success, evidence of the principal means of transport of that trade, boats, is of particular interest and importance. Many fragments of these ships have been recovered in London, usually reused in later structures, often in revetments. In one particular case, however, an almost complete boat was found buried in the river near Blackfriars in 1970. It was found just to the west of the foot of Trig Lane during the construction of the road beneath Blackfriars Bridge which extends some way out into the old river inside a caisson built to keep out the river. The ship was called 'Blackfriars 3' as four ships were found during these works: one Roman, one seventeenth-century and two medieval. The 'Blackfriars 3' ship was locally built, probably between 1380 and 1415 from dendrochronological analysis, and sank between 1480 and 1500 (Marsden 1994; Marsden 1996).

The ship was clinker-built of oak and was about 14.64m long, 4.3m wide and 0.9m high. It probably had a mast carrying a square sail and was thought to have been able to carry about 7.5 tonnes. It was probably pear-shaped, with the sharpest point at the bow, and was most probably a type of boat known as a 'shout'. Part of the bow was destroyed by the contractors and part of the starboard side still remains *in situ* beneath the river. The planks of the ship were fastened to the frames by use of willow or poplar trenails. Caulking between the planks was of matted goat hair and the rivets were of wrought iron. The base of the mast was square but its upper portions were presumably circular, about 0.18m in diameter, and it may have been about 8m high. Wear on the mast step clearly indicated that it had been removed regularly, presumably when the ship passed beneath low bridges. It may have been steered by a side oar given that it did not have a sternpost rudder, and side rudders are not known from medieval ships after the thirteenth century.

The ship was obviously designed to sail along the Thames and its tributaries and would have had a fairly wide reach in terms of the area it might have covered. Within it were found a total of 1,109 lead weights attached to a fibre, presumably a fishing net. This ship, however, was not a fishing vessel since no fish-well was found on it and thus presumably the fishing net had got trapped around the vessel. It was far more likely that this ship was a cargo carrier, not of stone, but of corn, tiles and other commodities.

Its sinking was, perhaps, the result of a collision with another boat, perhaps 'Blackfriars 4'. The two were found only a metre or two apart and lay as if they had hit each other. The 'Blackfriars 4' boat was carrying a load of ragstone which might perhaps have been a factor in causing a collision. It was considerably smaller than the 'Blackfriars 3' boat, suggesting that it was a lighter used for loading and unloading cargo from larger boats moored further out into the river.

Evidence of trade comes both from many groups of finds imported from the continent and from exported goods. One of England's principal industries was that of wool and cloth which fuelled the enormous increase of wealth in the fourteenth and fifteenth centuries. Although the wool trade declined in the fourteenth century, London's share of England's export market rose from 20 to 80 per cent. Lead cloth seals were placed on textiles from 1380 as a mark of their quality, and concentrations of seals on the foreshore may indicate where clothworkers were working. Perhaps the cloths were hung out to dry over the river walls and the seals dropped off into the river. The seals range from about 15mm to 30mm in diameter and have legends and heads upon them. Continental imports also illustrate that textiles were imported into London, for instance from Belgium and Venice (Egan *et al* 1998, 261–5). The cloth trade expanded enormously from 10,000 cloths in 1360 to 130,000 in the 1530s, and London's share of the national trade rose from 10 per cent to over 80 per cent (Barron in Palliser 2000, 412).

London Bridge

Documentary sources make clear that London Bridge was in constant need of repair and collapsed in places on a number of occasions (Watson *et al* 2001). One of the most serious collapses was in 1437 when the Stonegate and the arches on either side fell down. Evidence of the rebuilding works was found in the form of a dense area of elm piles driven into the foreshore to the north-west and south-east of the original abutment. An oak sill beam with holes on its underside was laid on the piles and attached to them. A new stone ashlar-faced wall, using similar stone and techniques as in the late twelfth-century wall, was then laid on the sill beam.

PALACES

Fewer new palatial structures were built during the latter part of the fourteenth century and during the fifteenth century but that in no way means that less money was lavished on the existing palaces by their owners. Most of the wealthier nobles and bishops already had a major London residence and there was little need to build another or replace the existing one. However, new fashions and increased retinues often meant that substantial extensions or alterations were made to some of London's grander houses. There were major developments in the palatial residences along Fleet Street in this period, including the destruction by fire of the Savoy and its rebuilding as a hospital by Henry VII in the early years of the sixteenth century, but little archaeological evidence of these houses has been recovered.

Fastolf's Place

In this period we do, however, have evidence of a major moated manor house from the central London area which replaced one previously held by Edward II. Documentary sources state that by 1376 the site of the Rosary on the south bank of the river, east of London Bridge (see chapter 3), had returned to the possession of the Dunleye family, who had originally sold the site to Edward II. At this time it contained houses and gardens enclosed with hedges and ditches, and two water mills. In 1442 Sir John Fastolf leased the entire property before buying it four years later. Fastolf demolished the mills and built himself a new house on the site in which he was living by 1450 at the time of Jack Cade's revolt. It is recorded that Fastolf garrisoned his Southwark house in order to destroy the Kentish rebels when they arrived in Southwark. In the event, when the rebels threatened to sack the house, Fastolf retreated with his private army across the river to the safety and security of the Tower of London. Fastolf died at Southwark in 1459 and after a long battle for the control of his estates his properties were granted to the Bishop of Winchester in 1472. A fairly detailed inventory of the estate survives from that time, describing the access to the property via a bridge and causeway crossing Fastolf's mill stream, the size of the moat surrounding the property, the gardens and specific details of the buildings within the moated enclosure. In 1484 the property was granted to the Earl of Nottingham. The inventory taken at that time lists many of the buildings mentioned in 1472, and also describes a wharf on the north side of the moat.

Later destruction meant that no evidence was recovered from any of the excavations for the 1440 phase of buildings at Fastolf's Place. The moat, however, did survive. It was found to have been revetted with timber on both banks. The moat appears to have silted up and been emptied, and the revetment had been repaired on a number of occasions. It was crossed by timber and earth causeways on both the east and west sides. To the east of the moat was part of a river inlet created by timber revetments. The end of this inlet was replaced in the fifteenth century by a stone river wall whose north face consisted of well-dressed ashlar ragstone. This also functioned as the northern wall of a long narrow building which was probably used as a warehouse for storage of goods transported by boats moored in the inlet.

Winchester Palace

There is also evidence for changes at two major ecclesiastical mansions – the Bishop of Winchester's house and the Archbishop of York's house – and two new major suites of monastic apartments were built – one for the Prior of St John of Jerusalem and the other for the Abbot of Westminster. Alterations to the bishop's house at Winchester occurred in the south and east ranges (Seeley in prep). A trapezoidally shaped garderobe, over 2.5m long, was inserted in the east range between the two rooms between 1320 and 1500. It was filled with layers of organic material containing food debris such as fish bone and animal bone. Lenses of lime were deposited periodically in the pit to lessen the smell. A deep foundation built on the outside of the east wall to the southern room may have been the base for a fireplace.

A final phase of construction involved the building of two rooms to the east and south of the ranges. Both rooms had less substantial foundations, perhaps implying single-storey structures, and were about 3m square. The northern room had a tiled floor bedded on a layer of mortar and stone chippings. Dating of this phase of activity is unclear but they were clearly additions to the thirteenth-century east range.

East of the east range lay the bishop's privy garden. Documentary evidence indicates that the bishop built a range of buildings in 1356–7 to act as his own personal apartments on the north side of this garden. As was usual, the principal rooms lay at first-floor level. This range was built to offer the bishop greater seclusion than that offered by the Great Hall and is typical of fourteenth-century attempts to provide greater privacy and increased levels of comfort in manorial, royal and ecclesiastical establishments. Similar examples can be seen in abbots' residences at many medieval monasteries, such as at Westminster.

A new waterfront was built about 4m to the south of the mid-thirteenth-century revetment from trees felled in 1354. This was a back-braced structure. An oak baseplate with grooves was laid, and inserted into these was a continuous line of vertical staves which would have been about 2m high, similar to that found at Trig Lane. These staves were supported by triangular braces on the landward side towards their tops and bases. The staves had all been removed during the construction of later waterfront structures but their impressions could still be seen. Two elm posts held the baseplate in place to prevent it from slipping out into the river. Material dumped behind the revetment included pottery, glass, leather, building material, animal bone and other artefacts – all, doubtless, discarded from the bishop's house. Interestingly, the material dumped behind the revetments dates to the end of the medieval period, either the late fifteenth or early sixteenth century, some 150 years or so after the revetment was constructed. In the city, dumping behind revetments always seems to have been carried out immediately the structure was built. This raises the possibility that this Winchester Palace revetment was in fact originally joined to the land by a wooden stage. This may have been a wharf or jetty along the river used by the Bishops of Winchester, and perhaps the floor of the jetty was removed during the early sixteenth century and the material dumped behind it shortly before the construction of a major river wall in the second half of the sixteenth century.

Archbishop of York's House

The Archbishop of York's house (at modern-day Whitehall Gardens) was extensively rebuilt in the fifteenth century, as many of the great bishops' houses were, and this is thought most likely to have taken place during the Archbishopric of George Neville (1465–76) (Thurley 1999). Much of the work was carried out in brick and stone, retaining some of the earlier buildings but demolishing many, probably those in timber. In essence the works consisted of a new range built to the south of the existing hall with a second hall to the east of both. North of the fourteenth-century hall was a cloister which was bounded by buildings on all sides: to the east a chamber and to the north the Great Hall. East of the chamber lay the existing chapel which was retained. Many of these buildings survived to a remarkable height, more than 1.5m, incorporated into the fabric of later buildings and it is a great pity that modern archaeological techniques were not available then to record them.

The major alterations to the existing hall were the demolition of the east wall and the insertion of a passage at the east end with a tiled floor. The range to the south of the hall contained at least two rooms, the eastern of which measured about 8m by 5.5m and had two windows in its southern wall. This south range, the halls and chambers are likely to have formed the residential areas of the house for the main occupants and their guests.

The public areas of York House were sited to the north and the cloister was built to maintain access between them. The Great Hall lay on the north side of the cloister next to the public areas and was a ground-floor hall. The Great Hall at Westminster was also of a single storey and lay in a similar position. The 'lesser hall' at Westminster and the existing hall at York House were both two-storey buildings and were essentially residential in character and not entered by the general public. This suggests that in a grand house the hall where public business was carried out was situated at ground-floor level while the residential dining hall was situated at first-floor level. A rectangular projection at the south, upper, end of the hall may have been the foundation for an oriel window, consistent with that seen in other houses of this date. The plans of grand houses, particularly those of the ecclesiastics, exhibit many similarities, with Lambeth Palace – the London residence of the Archbishops of Canterbury, situated on the opposite bank of the Thames to Westminster – akin to York House. Often these houses would have a residential hall at the southern end with a cloister attached, leading to a chapel on one side and apartments on the other. A great hall would often form the focus to the public areas of the house with a large open outer yard entered by a gate. Other domestic buildings such as kitchen, bakehouse, brewhouse and stables would have been arranged around the complex for ease of use, often the stabling being more peripheral and closer to the gates, whereas the kitchens were usually situated closer to the dining hall.

Prior of St John of Jerusalem's Residence

One new ecclesiastical residence was that of the Prior of St John of Jerusalem, who was one of the most powerful and influential nobles in the land. These apartments were built on the north side of the church in the latter part of the fourteenth century (Sloane and Malcolm in prep). On the west side of a courtyard lay a rectangular stone building. Initially the surveyors laid out the west wall at the wrong angle and the foundation trench had to be redug immediately. In total the range ran for at least 46m north of the chancel, and possibly as much as 62.5m, and it was 7.6m wide. Evidence for two rooms at the southern end of the range was found, the rooms being divided by a stone partition wall. Initially the northern room had a mortar floor which was subsequently relaid in clay. The southern room was reached by a doorway from the north some 2m wide. The room too was initially floored in mortar which was relaid in clay and in addition there was clear evidence that the walls had been plastered. Attached to the east wall of the range was a garderobe tower with a cesspit. Another cesspit added on to the east side between the two rooms indicates another garderobe chamber. The two rooms were eventually divided by a passage and the northern room was given a tiled floor, reusing old tiles of 'Westminster' and Penn type. A masonry cellar was also built against the west wall of the building in the late fifteenth century.

The lower rooms in this range, at least initially, were likely to have been fairly low-status, perhaps used for storage, while the upper two floors, identifiable from Hollar's view of the range which still stood in the seventeenth century, formed a hall and doubtless other chambers essential to an important baron like the prior, such as bed-chamber, dining halls and perhaps even an audience chamber. A fragment of another large wall to the east at the north end of the range seen in 1900 may perhaps be part of another east–west aligned range to the north of the church. A further range probably enclosed the courtyard on the east side leading back down to the church.

Abbot of Westminster's Residence

The other monastic apartments of great note are those of the Abbot at Westminster. In the place of the cellarer's buildings on the west side of the cloister, Abbot Littlyngton built himself and his successors a palatial new residence in the second half of the fourteenth century, including two rooms known as the Jerusalem Chamber and the Jericho Parlour. It is one of the finest suites of monastic accommodation built in late medieval England and still standing today. The buildings surrounded their own small courtyard which lay in the centre of the block (Fig. 50).

Edward III's Manor

We also know something of the layout and works at two royal houses of this period. A royal manor was established further along the south bank of the Thames at Rotherhithe. This was the moated manor of Edward III (1327–77), partially excavated on a site known as Platform Wharf (Blatherwick in prep). Initial recording of standing walls was carried out here in 1907 by Philip Norman, who found the north wall of a substantial medieval building still standing to 6m in height. Regrettably this was demolished when a tobacco warehouse was built but subsequent excavations found the wall standing almost to modern ground level and the other remains have been preserved in situ. This means that only limited amounts of the site have been excavated but these do give a fascinating insight into one of the lesser royal houses.

The site for Edward III's house was bought by the Crown by 1349. The house comprised a principal inner court which fronted on to the river and was surrounded by a moat, a stone wall built in 1353–4 and a timber palisade built around the moat (presumably along its outer edge) in 1356. The inner court would have contained the principal buildings. These included the hall (which documents tell us contained a fireplace), the kitchen (which the same sources describe as being built of stone with a timber roof and tiles paving the floor), and the king's chamber and chapel. Other chambers probably situated in the inner court were those of Roger Mortimer, John de Beauchamp, Robert Mauley and the lord prince. There was also a wharf reached by a bridge for access to the house by river. To the south of the moated inner court was an outer court which was enclosed by earth banks. It contained other buildings and a timber gatehouse. At the death of Edward III the house was given to the Abbey of St Mary Graces who leased it to Bermondsey Priory.

The moat surrounding the inner court was between 9.5m and 10.5m wide and up to 1.8m deep. A line of wooden posts along a step in the moat may have been either some form of revetment or perhaps a defensive palisade. The inner edge of the moat was formed by the outer wall of the inner court. The main entrance to the inner court was probably through a gatehouse in a tower in the north-west corner. It faced the river and may have led to the bridge to the river wharf. Parts of the walls of a tower were uncovered; the north wall was 1m thick while the west wall was a colossal 2.5m thick, and perhaps contained a staircase within its thickness.

A second entrance to the building must have led to the outer court on the south side, and evidence of this was found in the form of steps in the southern wall opposite where timbers were recorded in the fill of the moat, possibly from a bridge.

Although only limited excavation has taken place within the inner court, some information is known from both archaeological and documentary sources. The inner court measured some 30.5m north–south by 19.5m east–west with a structure, interpreted as the foundations of a tower, projecting 1.5m from the north-west corner of the building and 1m west of the western wall into the moat. The walls were constructed of fine ashlar blocks to plinth level with an irregularly coursed rubble superstructure.

The northern wall survived to a higher level. Despite being heavily truncated since it was recorded by Philip Norman in 1907, sills to the central two of the recorded lower openings were recorded *in situ*. Norman had not been able to record these as they were beneath the contemporary ground surface. Such a survival, even without the upper part of the wall recorded in 1907, is still remarkable. What the records show are windows at both ground-floor and first-floor level, with the former being larger and the latter closer together. The sills of the ground floor were made from Caen stone while the embrasure of the window was in greensand. Holes for the mullions indicate that the windows were each two lights wide and these were further subdivided into two by iron bars.

The other three sides of the court survived less well but were built in similar fashion. Within the ashlar facing of the west wall was a small arch which may have served as an outlet for the inner court's drainage system. About 5m north was a second opening, possibly fulfilling the same function.

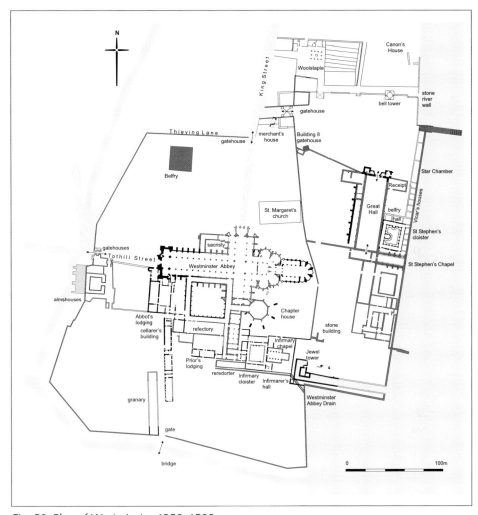

Fig. 50. Plan of Westminster 1350–1500

Palace of Westminster

Major changes were also carried out in the Palace of Westminster in the late fourteenth century (Fig. 50) (Thomas *et al* in prep). With the completion of St Stephen's Chapel during the reign of Edward III a college was formed to run it. This consisted of thirteen vicars whose houses were laid against the river, from the chapel to the north end of the Great Hall, and a dean and 12 canons whose house lay outside the palace, also alongside the river. The vicars' stone houses were of two storeys and fronted on to a two-storey cloister on the east side next to the chapel and a courtyard further north. The cloister was rebuilt in the early sixteenth century and still stands largely intact after repairs made following bomb damage in the Second World War. On the north side of the cloister the vicars had their own communal eating hall next to the belfry at first-floor level, with a kitchen, buttery and pantry on the ground floor beneath. The courtyard to the north was entered by a gate which led out into the public court: New Palace Yard. The canons each had a house of stone, perhaps with a timber-framed first floor. A vaulted drain ran under these houses exiting under the southernmost house into the river. These houses were built on land reclaimed from the river and signalled the disuse of the old dock.

In 1355 the woolstaple, founded in the northern part of the palace precincts, was separated from the rest of the public court by a stone wall, and a large bell tower was constructed part way along the wall.

Towards the end of the fourteenth century it was decided to rebuild the Great Hall, or at least to renew its roof and to add towers on to the north end to create a grand ceremonial entrance from the public yard. William Yevele, the foremost architect of his day, raised the walls by 1.52m, added new towers and built great flying buttresses on the outside to support the weight of the new roof. This hammerbeam roof, built by Master Hugh Herland, still survives and covers the largest area of any medieval timber roof in a single span without the need for pillars. It is one of the finest examples of its type in the world. The floor level was raised and paved in Purbeck marble, while statues of the kings of England were carved and placed in niches around the inside of the hall. A new range of buildings, incorporating the earlier barons' chamber, was added on to the west side of the hall. While these and the great exchequer have been demolished, the current late nineteenth-century buildings lie roughly on the original sites.

A new great gate was also built for Richard II in 1398, replacing the old gate into the yard. At this time the probable alehouse to the north of the gate underwent changes with the cesspit infilled and slots for beams indicating that the building was subdivided by partition walls. There is no reason to believe, however, that its use changed fundamentally. New stone yard surfaces were laid in the public yard, New Palace Yard, and a grand fountain was built in its centre, from which wine flowed at the coronation of the ten-year-old Richard II in 1377. It had an octagonal base fed by a drain; fragments of the demolished superstructure and drawings from the seventeenth century suggest it had a highly decorative, ornamental stone canopy (Horsman and Davidson 1989).

In 1365 Edward III purloined part of the abbey's precincts for his new Jewel Tower. This entailed rebuilding the abbey's boundary wall as well. The Jewel Tower, an L-shaped building four storeys high, still stands and was surrounded by a moat in which fish were kept (Fig. 51). It is recorded that the monks'

Fig. 51. The Jewel Tower and its moat (photo: MoLAS)

displeasure at having part of their precinct taken away from them was partly assuaged when the constable of the Jewel Tower choked to death on a fish bone from one of the fish in the moat – much to the monks' delight. The moat was probably crossed by a timber bridge and a set of stairs led down into it (Green 1976).

Further south, on a higher piece of ground in the marshes, lay one of Westminster's most peculiar finds. Here, where Elverton Street now lies, was a horse burial ground (Fig. 52). The horses, and indeed a large number of dogs, were buried in pits cut into the natural sand. The purpose of such a burial ground is unclear – the horses had not been butchered and eaten so perhaps they were considered too important to eat and might have been royal or nobles' hunting horses (Cowie and Pipe 1999).

The demise of the palace as a royal residence was the result of a disastrous fire in 1512 after which Henry VIII moved his seat of government up the road to Whitehall. Henry had a fondness for grand palaces that no other king seems to have been able to match. Retaining his other residences such as his palace at

Fig. 52. A burial pit from the horse burial ground at Elverton Street (photo: MoLAS)

Richmond, he also had built enormous new houses, for instance at Hampton Court and Nonsuch. The House of Lords, however, continued to sit in the Palace of Westminster, and from 1547 the House of Commons, which had usually sat in the abbey infirmary or chapter house, also sat in the palace in the former St Stephen's Chapel, sealing the transition of the palace from the monarch's seat to the seat of Parliament.

RELIGION

England and its people were still influenced enormously by the Church in the later medieval period but the domination of the Catholic Church came under increasing threat. There were also a number of significant changes to religious beliefs, in particular the rise of the doctrine of purgatory. This conveniently explained to layfolk the limbo in which the dead were held and thus reinforced the punishment to be expected by sinners – although by its very nature, all those who went to purgatory were bound for heaven and not hell. The upshot was the desire for those able to afford it to found chantry chapels in which masses could be held in their name, thus reducing their time in purgatory. Other charitable deeds and acts might result in an individual being the recipient of a papal bulla, also thought to save the individual's soul from some time in purgatory. This was a document with a lead seal attached which was given by the Church in recognition of an individual's works. The obvious importance attributed to them by the owners is clear. Skeletons are often found with the lead seal, sometimes even clutched in the hand as if the individuals concerned were desperate to carry it with them as proof of their good deeds.

During the fourteenth century there was a change in attitude to the provision of charity to the poor. Charity was now distributed to the 'deserving poor' and thus new almshouses were built to provide care for such groups as blind priests, retired seamen or retired members of the city guilds. These almshouses were usually built on the claustral pattern with individual houses built around a cloister and a small chapel attached on the eastern side. This change in provision of care did not stop the main hospitals that had already been established from taking in the sick and the destitute; it merely meant that there were no new foundations to cater for them.

Parish Churches

Regrettably, little archaeological evidence of parish churches in the city from the late medieval period survives, although documentary sources make clear that money was spent on new belfries and towers on some existing churches. Some evidence of further rebuilding at St Nicholas Shambles was found but once again only truncated foundations which date to either the fourteenth, fifteenth or early sixteenth century. The north aisle (see chapter 3) was extended to the east end of the second chancel, making it the full length of the church. At some time the east end of the chancel was also rebuilt and it seems likely that this happened at the same time as the extension of the north aisle (Riviere in White 1988, 8).

Religious houses

Many monastic houses owned large tracts of property in the countryside and tenements in the city and suffered acutely after the Black Death owing to the fall in their property values. There does, however, seem to have been a renaissance in their fortunes more often than not in the fifteenth century. This is commonly characterised by the increasing secularisation and development of their outer precincts, which filled up with tenements, mansions, traders and artisans.

Abbey of St Mary Graces

Two new large monastic houses were founded during this period, both on the sites of the former Black Death cemeteries. One was the Cistercian Abbey of St Mary Graces at East Smithfield, the other the London Charterhouse, a Carthusian monastery, at West Smithfield. Both are unusual in that Cistercian houses were usually founded in the twelfth or early thirteenth century and had become relatively unpopular as new foundations by the second half of the fourteenth century, while Carthusian houses are rare in England as a whole and were normally rural rather than urban. There were only nine Carthusian monasteries in England but some of the second wave of foundations do seem to have been urban.

Edward III founded the Abbey of St Mary Graces in 1350 for twenty-four monks but the monastery was relatively impoverished and barely ever achieved half that number. It does not appear to have had a contingent of lay brothers, which although usual in Cistercian houses is not surprising given the large fall in their numbers at the other Cistercian houses in the fourteenth and fifteenth centuries (Grainger *et al* in prep).

A fragmentary section of wall which was abutted by the early cloisters is thought to have been the original Black Death chapel founded in 1349 for masses to be said for the victims buried there. This building was reused at first as the monastic church and subsequently remained in use as a chapel, perhaps for the entire monastic period. The cloisters lay to the south of the chapel and were separated from it by a lane. They measured 29m east–west by 20m north–south internally and were surrounded by covered alleys. The lane between the cloisters and the church is unknown in other British Cistercian houses and suggests the influence of friaries which often had lanes to allow the laity access to the preaching churches while giving the cloister a greater air of seclusion. Perhaps lay folk were permitted to worship in the chapel because of its origin as the Black Death chapel.

Construction of a new church began in 1361 and to the south were built the usual accompanying buildings such as the frater and the chapter house. These were never situated around the early cloister, however, giving the plan a most unusual appearance. The chancel of the church was a simple structure 24m long and 7m wide, with twenty-four graves under the floor. Some of the graves contained tomb structures and grave slabs and one burial had been decapitated, the axe marks showing in the vertebra. Documentary evidence of the location of this burial indicates that it was of Sir Simon Burley, executed on Tower Hill in 1388. The nave appears to have been added to the chancel; it was 18.5m wide and less than 25m long. Piers divided the nave into central, north and south aisles. A large number of burials were found in the nave. All sexes and ages were represented, although a substantial majority were adults and there were more males than females. The south aisle was the most popular area for burial. A chapel was later created at the east end of the south aisle and a rood screen was built across the eastern bay of the nave. The chapel was separated from the nave by a timber screen and it was floored in tiles. Two graves may have had above-ground monuments and both had a second burial placed into them at a later date, partly disturbing the original skeleton. One of these was buried with a poorly preserved lead papal bulla on its chest, tentatively dated to the pontificate of anti-pope Clement VIII of Avignon in 1424–9. Abutting the north side of the chancel was a building which can probably be identified as the Lady Chapel.

The chapter house was built to the south of the church between 1365 and 1375 and was a simple rectangular building of 12.75m by 6m internally. The exterior of the wall was faced in coursed ragstone and the interior in coursed chalk. Fragments of a bench or foot rest were found against the inside edges of the walls and it originally had a tiled floor.

To the south of the nave, in the yard formed by the wall running south from the chancel, was evidence for the cloister. This mainly consisted of some badly truncated wall foundations which may have been part of the lavatorium. A stone wall perhaps represented part of the east alley of a set of cloisters or perhaps just a covered way past the chapter house to the church. There was also a timber pentice along the south side of the nave, suggesting a covered passageway not dissimilar to the north walk of a cloister. Both structures contained burials, with the northern pentice containing a high proportion of young people (albeit from a very small sample of eight). There was no other evidence for cloister alleys (Grainger *et al* in prep).

To the south of the south-west cloisters lay buildings identified as the kitchen and a store-room. The frater or refectory lay in the traditional siting for a Cistercian frater, that is, south of the church and at right angles to a putative cloister. A large buttress on the west side may have been the foundation for the pulpit from which biblical passages were read at meal times, and there was evidence of a dais at the south end. Two fragments of tiled floor were also found. The building measured almost 19.5m by 7.25m and the south wall survived to an impressive 2.20m in height, showing that the wall was faced in chalk on the inside and ragstone with bands of flint on the outside. To the west of the frater and running southwards for some 40m to the edge of the site was a vaulted chalk drain. No sign of the monks' dormitory was found but the walls of the infirmary were recovered. This building was documented as being built in 1391–2 and lay immediately to the south of the chapter house. The eastern wall survived to some 2m above its construction level. A door in the southern wall may have been an original feature, as may have been one in the east wall. A fireplace, nearly 3m wide, was built in the east wall as part of the original construction. The building was divided at ground-floor level by a stone wall. There was also clear evidence of stone tenements in the precinct, as has been found at most of the other monastic houses of the period.

The churchyard of St Mary Graces covered the northern part of the western burial area within the Black Death cemetery, and included an area not previously used for burial. In total 305 burials were found in the cemetery and these fell into two basic patterns, but all were buried in the traditional manner – on their backs with their heads at the west end. The first pattern consisted of twenty rows of burials both over and between the Black Death burial areas. Some of the second pattern of burials were later and comprised eight groups of sixty graves containing sixty-two individuals buried somewhat haphazardly rather than in neat rows. Again the overwhelming majority were adults and, of those that could be sexed, more were male than female.

Charterhouse

The London Charterhouse became the fourth monastic house in the north-western suburb of London in 1372, built on lands owned by St Bartholomew's

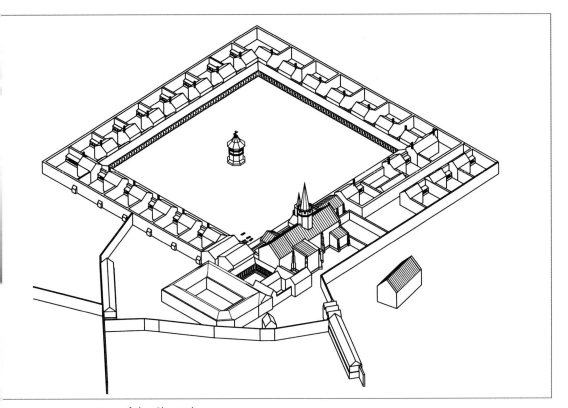

Fig. 53. Reconstruction of the Charterhouse

and St John's. Carthusian monasteries differed from the other monasteries in an important way. The monks led a hermit-like solitary lifestyle of almost total silence which led to them having a large cloister around which were built individual cells for each monk (Fig. 53). The cells were entered by a doorway next to which was a hatch through which food could be given to each monk. A bend in the hatch meant that no contact could be made between the monk and the attendant who left the food. The cells were of two storeys and were surrounded by an L-shaped garden. The cell door opened on to a narrow corridor with a tiled floor that led to the two main ground-floor rooms where the monk slept and worked. It also led to a wider corridor which lay parallel to the cloister alley. This too had a tiled floor while the main rooms were floored in mortar. A second corridor led away from the cell building to a latrine with a tap along the wall to provide water. A wall surrounded the cell and its garden where the monk could grow plants. As with all monasteries a water supply was of vital importance. A remarkable fifteenth-century map shows the water supply coming from the north to a great conduit in the centre of the cloister, from which supplies were taken to each cell and the other main buildings. The main supply was fed by a lead pipe, as were the supplies from the conduit (Barratt and Thomas 1991; Barber and Thomas 2002).

After bombing in 1941 had severely damaged the Charterhouse mansion which replaced the monastery, extensive excavations led to the recovery of the ground plan of the original church, which previous writers had mistakenly assumed to be where the current chapel now stands. Once the excavators had realised that the monastic church must lie elsewhere, they excavated the likely site of the high altar and of the tomb of the founder, Sir Walter Manny, who would have been buried near it. They judged that a squint (or window) in the adjacent tower looked down on to the high altar and excavation proved this to be the case. They also found a tomb containing a lead coffin, inside which was the skeleton of a man whose red hair still survived. Clutched in his hand was a papal bulla which was confirmed as belonging to Manny. It is now known that the post-dissolution chapel lies over the original chapter house. The little cloister lay to the west of the church, surrounded by buildings including the guest-house. West of the little cloister lay the Wash-house Court which still stands today. This was built in about 1519 as accommodation for the *conversi* or lay brothers. The buildings were constructed from red brick which was by that time becoming more popular and widely used in London. Diaper patterning in the walls can also be seen in the precinct wall to the west which must be of a similar date. A range of stone buildings and a yard inside a large stone wall to the north-west indicate the probable extent of the 'inner court', which no doubt contained the necessary buildings for the maintenance of daily life in a monastic house: barns, kitchens, bakehouse, brewhouse, etc. The main part of the precinct was entered by a gatehouse from Charterhouse Square, which was divided from the monastery by a stone wall. The square, originally the site of one of the Black Death burial grounds, could therefore be accessed by the public without them gaining entry to the rest of the precinct.

Holy Trinity Priory Aldgate

There is also abundant archaeological evidence from the pre-existing monastic houses in London. One of the most remarkable finds was of a chapel with an extraordinary, well-preserved standing arch at Holy Trinity Priory (Fig. 18). The chapel dates to between 1360 and 1400 and was entered by an arch which was originally constructed in the twelfth century (see chapter 2). The core of the wall was subsequently cut for the insertion of a new arch, which was two-centred and set on the earlier jambs. Two slots or cuts in each of the jambs may

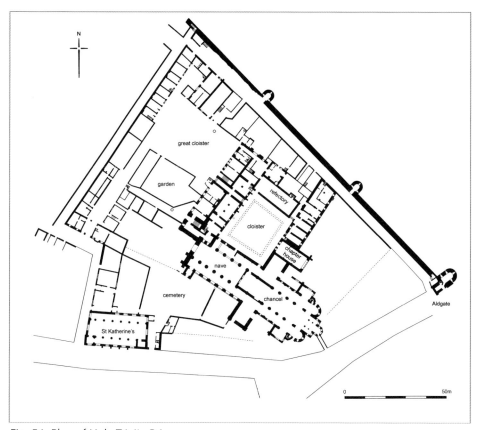

Fig. 54. Plan of Holy Trinity Priory

have supported horizontal timbers for a screen. To the east of the arch were the remains of a window. The likeliest date for this new arch is probably the same period as the wall foundations and therefore the second half of the fourteenth century (Schofield *et al* in prep). A reconstructed plan of the complex at this time is shown in Fig. 54.

Nunnery of St Clare

On the eastern side of the city lay the Franciscan nunnery of St Clare. This was originally founded in 1294 and attracted many wealthy and high-status female patrons. Two remarkable discoveries were made in 1964 and 1987. The second of these exposed one of the best-surviving medieval pieces of masonry yet to be found on an archaeological site in London. Behind the facing of the building on the site lay a two-storey medieval wall with doorways at ground-floor and first-floor level and a staircase joining them. The wall formed the western wall to a two-roomed structure south of the cloister. The find in 1964 was possibly even more dramatic. The Lady Chapel of the nunnery had been converted into the parish church of Holy Trinity Minories at the dissolution (the Minoresses was one of the names given to the Franciscan nuns and the name survives in the modern street) and this was only demolished in the early part of the twentieth century. When building works were carried out in 1964 part of the church was discovered and within it a vault containing the lead coffin of Anne Mowbray, daughter of the Duke of Norfolk and child bride of Richard, the younger of the princes allegedly murdered in the Tower in 1483. They were married when he was only four and she was five. She was nine when she died in 1481 but her high status granted her a fine burial. Her coffin was inscribed and, because it had been sealed, contained a remarkably preserved skeleton within it with large amounts of her red hair still surviving.

Priory and Hospital of St Mary Spital

Despite the fall in its wealth, St Mary Spital was able to carry out a campaign of building in the second half of the fourteenth century (Thomas *et al* 1997). A reconstruction of a part of the site is shown in Fig. 55. A stone house was built

Fig. 55. Reconstruction painting of St Mary Spital

for the lay sisters who looked after the sick, including a room for them in which to sleep and an eating area with a dais at one end for religious texts to be read during their meals. A stone porch led into the sleeping area and a door led into a hall in the middle of the building, with doors on either side into the dormitory and the refectory. This building was constructed next to the infirmary so as to make their access to the inmates more convenient. The building had only shallow foundations, indicating that it was only of one storey, and reused stone from demolished buildings in the area. The Copperplate Map of about 1550 shows the building still standing and that it had gables in the roof. Fragments of stone from later buildings on the site indicate that the windows had shutters. The fact that the lay sisters were the last of the establishment's staff to be given a stone building illustrates their low position, which is confirmed by documentary sources. These repeatedly show that the lay sisters were not receiving their due allocations of money and food. They had their own garden with a stone well and they dug pits to dispose of their rubbish in the garden. During the fifteenth century their garden was divided from the kitchen garden, and their refectory was linked by a corridor to the kitchen, as scandal had been reported to the Bishop of London concerning the sisters consorting with males at the monastery.

A new Lady Chapel was built at the east end of the church in about 1400 and many fragments of stone from the windows and columns that adorned it have been recovered. The south aisle was extended shortly afterwards and a new chapel created. The small amount that has been excavated suggests that it was used for the burial of young children. Because the east wall of this chapel was reused as the boundary to a garden in the post-dissolution period, it survived to a remarkable height, immediately beneath the modern road surface.

In front of the charnel house were two tombs where high-status individuals wished to be buried so that they would be noticed by visitors to the chapel. Perhaps one belonged to the founder of a chantry in the chapel, William Eynsham. The other contained the skeleton of a woman buried with a papal bulla and was probably that of his wife Johanna. In the middle of the cemetery stood an open-air pulpit whose walls, like those of the charnel house, were adorned with flint and stone decoration, possibly in a chequerboard pattern. From this pulpit, sermons were read to throngs of people who gathered in the cemetery at Easter. A gallery was built for the Lord Mayor and aldermen so that they could listen to the sermons in comfort and be seen by the general populace.

Many thousands of people continued to be buried in the cemetery right up to the closure of the hospital in 1539. Large numbers of diseased individuals have been recovered, some showing evidence of tuberculosis and syphilis. At least two individuals also had leprosy; lepers were specifically banned from the hospital by the statutes but clearly these individuals went unnoticed. There were many with healed fractures, at least one case of an amputation and two incidences of trepanning (a surgical procedure where holes were drilled in the skull as a cure for epilepsy). Both of the individuals who had been trepanned survived the operation, as there was regrowth of bone over part of the holes. This suggests that more complex medical practices, perhaps including surgery, were being carried out at the hospital in the later medieval period.

In the southern part of the precincts, houses were built for residents at the hospital who received free board and lodging in return for granting the hospital all their goods when they died. Their houses were timber-framed on stone foundations and each had a small garden at the back with a cesspit. They took their water from communal wells and received a diet of broth, bread, ale, fish and meat. The houses fronted on to a road which ran through the precinct, somewhat similar to that at St John's in Clerkenwell (see below). The increased secularisation of the precincts is graphically illustrated by the fact that one of these houses was lived in by a prostitute, Joan Jolybody, not the sort of activity normally associated with the precincts of a monastic house.

St Mary Clerkenwell

Until the end of the fifteenth century the nunnery at St Mary Clerkenwell was suffering serious financial problems, which, as with many major institutions, were caused by the fall in property values after the Black Death. For the first time the records tell us how many nuns were resident at the nunnery: fifteen in 1379 and seventeen four years later (Sloane in prep).

Alterations were made to some of the buildings, including the guests' hall and the kitchen, and a new building was constructed in the service courtyard; although little of its interior has been excavated, its association with stone- and tile-lined drains has tentatively identified it as a wash-house. Part of the precinct wall was found in the 1920s when work was carried out on the Clerk's Well. A gap in the wall was presumably designed to allow water through from the spring. This was blocked up and refaced in brick when a brick and stone wall was built some 2m from the precinct wall, forming a tank. Three stone steps led down into the tank into which the spring water flowed. A brick overflow drain, floored in Flemish tiles, led down towards the River Fleet.

By the end of the fifteenth century the nunnery's fortunes seem to have taken a turn for the better. Considerable expenditure was made in particular on the

Fig. 56. Reconstruction of the interior of the church at St Mary Clerkenwell

main religious areas, namely the church, which was being rebuilt in 1478, and the cloister, rebuilt in the sixteenth century. The plan of the church did not alter, although its north wall was rebuilt, new windows were inserted at the east end and in the tower, and the roof was rebuilt at a lower level. A reconstruction of this is shown in Fig. 56. Substantial rebuilding of the cloister and its ranges did, however, occur, including a new cellar immediately adjacent to the refectory. Part of the south walk still survives to the north of the eighteenth-century church. The cloister measured about 29m by 25m but was slightly irregular in shape, with seven bays in the northern and southern walks and only

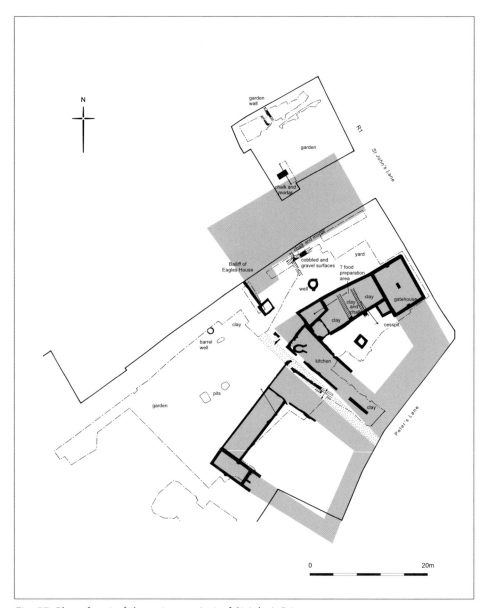

Fig. 57. Plan of part of the outer precinct of St John's Priory

six in the eastern and western. It was probably covered by a shallow lean-to roof and floored in plain-glazed Flemish tiles set diagonally to the walls.

Building works on the kitchen also seem to have been more active in the late fifteenth and sixteenth centuries. A new partition wall and replacement hearths were inserted. Again there was plentiful evidence for the meat part of the diet, including ox, sheep/goat, pig, brown hare, rabbit, chicken, duck, goose, grey partridge, swan and woodcock. The variety of fish eaten seems to have increased but, as was seen at St Mary Spital, herring seems to have become less popular at this time, with eel replacing it.

Priory of St John Clerkenwell

Two major changes occurred at the priory of St John's in Clerkenwell in the later medieval period (Sloane and Malcolm in prep). First, the inner precinct, and in particular the area to the north of the church, was rebuilt as a major residence for the prior who had become an important member of the nobility (see above). Secondly, the outer precinct was developed on a very large scale and along with St Mary Spital provides us with the most extensively excavated evidence for the use of a monastic outer precinct in later medieval London (Fig. 57). To turn first to the developments in the inner precinct, the church was provided with a north aisle at some time around the middle of the fourteenth century and the windows were replaced in the church in the mid-fifteenth century. A beautiful chapel was also built south of the chancel for the prior Thomas Dowcra who died in 1527. Arched openings led into it from the church and many fine stone mouldings indicate how remarkably well decorated this chapel was.

To the west of the southern end of the main north–south range of the prior's apartments lay the great chamber, parts of the undercroft of which still survive. Projecting out from it was the great stair. Further west, parts of another undercroft were found when the standing buildings on the north side of St John's Square were refurbished. This building is interpreted as being the undercroft to the Great Hall. The undercroft consisted of at least four chambers, probably service rooms, containing evidence of windows and one complete medieval doorway. A stone corbel in one room indicates that there was a wooden floor above, giving headroom of at least 2.3m. The ground level was at least 0.5m lower than this corbel, suggesting that a flight of stairs must have led up to the Great Hall above. Documentary evidence indicates that the hall was 32m long and 12m wide, with its main entrance at the western end. Adjacent to the west end stood the kitchen which was next to the Yeomen's Dormitory, parts of which were found early in the twentieth century.

Two areas of cemetery have been identified: one adjacent to the long range to the north of the chancel and one to the south of the church, but only very small numbers of burials have been excavated. The area to the north of the church included men, women and children, and so does not appear to have been set aside for burials of the brethren exclusively. One female still retained her foetus, indicating that she had died in childbirth. The burying of pregnant women was

Fig. 58. St John's Priory gatehouse (photo: MoL)

contrary to the decrees of the Council of Canterbury (1236) and the Council of Trèves (1310) which stated that it was unlawful to bury a woman until the foetus had been removed (Anderson and Parfitt 1998, 123), but, as at St Mary Spital where the same practice was carried out, this was clearly not adhered to.

The most instantly recognisable building today is the great gate to the inner precinct which still stands complete although with later alterations, particularly where it has been refaced (Fig. 58). Above the south side of the gate arch are the arms of Prior Thomas Dowcra and the date of 1504. Two gate towers, 8.5m by 4.4m internally, lie on either side of the gate arch which was passed under by a gravel road. The road level was about 1m below where it stands today. The gate towers had five storeys including an undercroft and extended to a height of just over 16m above the original construction level. The undercroft walls are masonry, very much larger than the brick walls above, and are thought to have been part of an earlier gate on the site. The brick walls above ground were faced in ragstone, a somewhat peculiar design given the rise in the status of brick buildings at this time. The arch span was nearly 6.5m wide and 7.25m high, and the arch had a total length of 7.8m. One hinge survives, indicating where the original gates hung. The western tower has a stair turret which had a stone stair from the ground floor and a timber stair above. There are two rooms at the ground-floor level and a garderobe. Above the arch lies a grand room almost 6.5m square, accessible from either gate tower and with large traceried windows to both north and south.

Major developments took place in the outer precinct to the south of the great gate. A gravel road linked the great gate to a stone outer gate which replaced the earlier timber version. The first stone gate was almost entirely replaced but enough survived to show that the western side was constructed from chalk blocks and had a clay floor. It was again rebuilt, perhaps after the damage caused by the Peasants' Revolt in 1381. Its western tower was also found; it measured 8.8m by 6.4m and had a vaulted undercroft built from chalk. A central column base and a southern respond supported the vaulted ceiling, and the floors were also laid in chalk. A cesspit was attached to the outside of the gatehouse, possibly serving a garderobe.

A gravel track led westwards from the main road through the precinct to the hospital croft. South of this road was a building which measured at least 17m by 4m and was probably timber-framed on shallow stone footings. It contained at least two rooms of which the eastern contained two sunken hearths in a clay floor. The western room had probably been tiled as a substantial number of 'Westminster' and Penn decorated floor tiles were found in the demolition rubble. This structure may have been a tenement in the outer precinct, perhaps for one of the officers of the Bailiff of Eagle, who was an important official of the priory (originally the bailiff of a Templar preceptory at Eagle in Lincolnshire).

In the south-west corner of the precinct on the west side of an alley lay the fragmentary remains of a building which perhaps surrounded a courtyard and was presumably a domestic tenement. Overall it measured 22.5m by at least 10m and had stone footings for timber-framed walls above. The north-western range measured nearly 13m by 4m and had a cellar on its eastern side. It was rebuilt at a later date when it may have had a tiled floor. A large amount of debris, interpreted as stable waste, was deposited in the cellar at this time. On the eastern side of the courtyard lay a building which had stone or stone-founded walls on three sides but was open with timber posts on the fourth, suggesting that it may have been the stable from which the stable waste originated. At around the time when the stable waste was dumped, the building may have ceased use as a stable and its site used for pit digging for rubbish disposal.

On the eastern side of the same alley lay another building ranged around a courtyard. Subsequent development of these buildings extended right up to the outer precinct gatehouse. The earliest phase comprised at least two rooms alongside the alley. One room measured at least 10m by 4m and had two entrances on to the alley to the west, and one to the east. Tiles of 'Westminster' and Penn type formed the floor. The southern room measured at least 5m by 2.5m. By the mid-fifteenth century the larger room had been partitioned. The other room had evidence of burning on the floor, perhaps indicating a hearth, and twenty-two iron nails and an iron frame from a shoe were found. A third room was added at the north end, at this time measuring about 5m by 3m. This was subsequently incorporated into a larger room measuring 8m by 5m. Next to it was built yet another room 13m long. The building was also extended eastwards to the gatehouse with another range. The stone walls had been robbed out but the floors of chalk and mortar survived in places.

In the mid-fifteenth century the main tiled room was altered when the doorways in the western wall were blocked, the southern partition was replaced (increasing the length of this room to 10m) and the tile floor was removed and replaced with a clay floor. A keyhole-shaped oven was built in the north corner of the room, made from roof tiles bonded with clay, indicating that this room had been turned into a kitchen. This building would seem to have been another tenement of some quality with domestic buildings arranged around a courtyard and evidence for halls, kitchens and other accommodation.

One other substantial tenement of quite high status built after 1500 was found within the precinct. It lay to the south-west of the gatehouse and consisted of eastern and western ranges with a building in between. The occupants of these houses were clearly wealthy and were perhaps merchants or well-to-do citizens. Most of the foundations were brick although they also reused masonry from demolished buildings in the precinct. The western range had only robbed-out foundations to show the layout of its walls. The eastern range survived much better with brick walls and floors laid in chalk and mortar. The northern building appears to have acted as a porch although it did have a semi-basement within it. One piece of terracotta mullion was found in one area and another seventy-five pieces were found in the footings of the post-dissolution building which occupied the site, suggesting that this building was decorated with them – in which case it was constructed in about 1515–25. These terracottas are highly unusual and are directly comparable to those from Layer Marney, a house in Essex. The house seems to have been in the ownership of Thomas Leyond at the time.

All in all, the activity at St John's gives a picture of an outer gate which led to a road through to the main inner precinct. Along the road were shops and working areas – for butchery and tilemaking among others – and a variety of tenements with their own gardens behind them, some owned by wealthier members of society who seem to have been attracted to these establishments in the latter years of the medieval period. They were obviously not attracted by a secluded atmosphere since this outer precinct, in common with the others excavated around London, was obviously a busy and bustling place with manufacturing and trading going on all around. Instead they may have been drawn by its proximity to the residence of the prior. His apartments lay to the north of the church, inside the great gate, and were of an even higher status, as befitting a very wealthy lord and landowner with a prominent position in society.

Bermondsey Priory

To the south of the Thames Bermondsey Priory, after the financial problems of the previous century, enjoyed an upturn in its fortunes during the later fourteenth and fifteenth centuries. This was aided by royal patronage and also by its being made an abbey in 1399 (Steele in prep). The burial of Henry V's queen, Katherine, in the Lady Chapel in 1437 was followed by other aristocratic burials, such as that of Ann, Lady Audley. The east end of the church appears to have been altered during the fourteenth century and fragments of stone indicate that traceried windows were inserted during the second half of that century.

Almost all of the infirmary, except for the east wall which was reused, and its service buildings were demolished in the fourteenth century to make way for a new infirmary complex. The old east wall became the new west wall of the structure, which was a rectangular building about 27m east–west by 16m north–south. Three rooms about 4.5m wide and at least 4.3m long led off its east end. The lack of surviving internal walls or floors makes it unclear whether the large space consisted of one hall or a variety of rooms with open yards between. The moulded stone recovered indicates that the buildings had shuttered windows of essentially domestic character. The new infirmary was bounded on its east side by an infirmary cloister with a cloister walk. Infirmary cloisters are common in fourteenth-century monasteries and are often part of a scheme of greater segregation for the individual monks (see Westminster Abbey below). In the south wall of the cloister walk was a well, which occupied a similar position in this cloister to the lavabo in the principal monastic cloister. In the north-west corner of the cloister garth was a small rectangular building.

A copper-alloy stamp from the later destruction of this building suggests it may have been used as a small scriptorium or office, for writing letters and official documents.

Alterations were made to the reredorter, and the main drain was robbed out, indicating that the reredorter became one large cesspit in the mid- to late fifteenth century. The large quantities of pottery found show unusual proportions of pottery fabrics, with Kingston ware, by now very much out of date, even more numerous than Coarse Border ware, suggesting that Kingston ware continued in use for much longer in Southwark than it did north of the river. The vessel forms are typical of those produced later in the life of the industry and many can be paralleled in the recently excavated early fourteenth-century kiln waste from Eden Street in Kingston upon Thames (Stephenson and Miller 1996, 72). These included a tulip-necked baluster jug, small rounded jugs, rilled baluster jugs and bowls. One particularly interesting aspect of this pottery is the large number of ceramic urinals which were recovered.

Only twenty-one interments were identified in the cemetery in the period up to the second quarter of the fifteenth century; after that the medieval cemetery appears to have undergone a change of use in the last hundred years of the abbey. In that time it was used for the digging of rubbish pits to dispose of waste. The pottery, most of which dates to the late fourteenth or fifteenth century, appears to represent a clear-out of unwanted equipment and utensils. This part of the cemetery was therefore no longer used for burial, implying that burials either continued in other parts of the cemetery, as yet unexcavated, or were confined to the church. This lack of interments in late monastic cemeteries has been seen elsewhere (for example at Stratford Langthorne Abbey) and is something of a puzzle. We know from documentary sources that diseases such as plague were taking a large toll on the population and this certainly affected monastic houses such as Westminster Abbey. So where are the burials from later monastic sites such as Bermondsey and Stratford? Certainly, the high degree of residuality in the pottery found in graves (that is, pottery from earlier periods that was dug up by the digging of the graves and redeposited in their backfills) is likely to bias the phasing of cemeteries towards the earlier periods but does this account for all of the apparent absence of burial or is there a change in burial location in the later medieval periods which means that we are, as yet, not finding these skeletons?

The private hall complex was again extended and reached a complete length of 32m. This structure might have provided two or more suites of accommodation for corrodians or wealthy tenants such as, perhaps, Queen

Katherine or Elizabeth Woodville, widows of Henry V and Edward IV respectively. This signals a change in the monastery, seen in the surviving documents, with increasing numbers of lay people living there. This is a common feature of monastic houses in London and indicates a relaxation in the attitudes to strict monastic life. The greater comfort and lavishness of the buildings is also a feature of this period and can be seen at many of the other monastic houses in London. The documents also indicate that the abbey was leasing or selling large parts of its estates, perhaps because the abbots could see the dissolution coming.

Westminster Abbey

The completion of the abbey church at Westminster, started by Henry III, took until the early sixteenth century, though the towers at the west end were finished and clad in Portland stone by Nicholas Hawksmoor much later, in the early eighteenth century. Of the final medieval parts of the abbey, perhaps the greatest was the new Lady Chapel. Known as the Henry VII chapel, it was built in the early years of the sixteenth century with a magnificent fan-vaulted ceiling and became a mausoleum for the Tudor and Stuart monarchs. Other major changes to the abbey at this time were made to the claustral buildings. A great fire in 1298 had seriously damaged the infirmary and this and other parts of the cloister were rebuilt during the abbacy of Nicholas Littlyngton in the third quarter of the fourteenth century (Fig. 50). Instead of building a great new infirmary hall, a cloister was built with the infirmary chapel of St Katherine on its east side. Around this cloister were built individual houses for the sick monks. This practice of increasing segregation can be seen in monastic dormitories, where screens divided the beds from one another, and in the new almshouses which had separate accommodation for each inmate. Indeed, such an almshouse was built at the turn of the sixteenth century on the west side of the abbey precincts. Littlyngton also demolished the old west range of the cloister and rebuilt the cellarer's buildings further south. These now formed the other side of a lane to the granary (see chapter 3).

The October Fair was in decline in the late fourteenth century and had ended by the late fifteenth century. This was possibly a result of the power of the city traders and the decline in fairs in general. Perhaps the October Fair was simply unable to compete. Changes which reflect this were seen in the merchants' building excavated near the north gate. Here the former path down the middle of the room went out of use and rows of posts show that the building was subdivided into separate rooms, divided by timber partitions. These were still floored in clay and mortar but the painted plaster was stripped from the walls and a small roof-tile hearth was inserted in the floor of the central room (Thomas *et al* in prep).

CONCLUSION: CHANGE AND DISSOLUTION

The fall in property prices after the Black Death had a serious economic effect upon London but this was soon overcome and the fifteenth century was a period of economic expansion which led to even greater opulence and a higher standard of living. It has been estimated that London's population was perhaps about 40,000 for much of this period, with only about 3,000 being citizens. With about 20,000 women, the other 17,000 were made up of children, clergy and labourers with no rights to political office. Nonetheless some of these labourers would have been able to earn a reasonable living (Barron in Palliser 2000, 400).

New alleys and lanes were built within the city to cater for the new migrants, while wealthier merchants were able to afford ever more extensive properties and affluent lifestyles. The urban sprawl probably did not extend significantly further during the later medieval period although there was further reclamation into the river and of the marshland to the north. The increasing migration into the city can be seen in the change in its mayors and aldermen. Where once certain families dominated these posts, now high office rarely passed from one generation to another and such posts were often held by people from out of London, such as Richard Whittington from Gloucestershire or Adam Fraunceys from Yorkshire.

The majority of houses were still timber-framed and the poorest sections of the community maintained a fairly poor lifestyle. The number of wealthy merchants, however, greatly increased and grand residences were built throughout the city on larger areas of ground, mimicking the mansions of the nobility and bishops. Some of these were stone-built throughout and may have contained tiled floors and upper storeys with solars and bedrooms with high-quality furnishings. Wealthier houses used glass vessels more and more, with some imported from Venice or Florence, and in some cases glass was actually produced by Venetian and Florentine makers in London. Metal cauldrons and other kitchen implements were also more common.

Recreational pastimes had obviously always been important but we can see in this period that Londoners spent some of their time listening to or playing music, playing chess or dice, practising archery or skating.

London's food supply probably became more complex and more based upon large-scale production from the hinterland, purchased by cash. New markets sprang up, such as the Leadenhall Garner, to cater for the increased trade. The docks were extended, and more secure and stable stone walls were built to provide adequate and safe harbour for the enormous number of vessels using the Thames. The inherently risky nature of seafaring and the large amount of river traffic obviously caused problems as shown by the sunken boats found at Blackfriars.

The government of England was more firmly established at Westminster but there was massive instability during the Wars of the Roses in the fifteenth century and nothing approaching stable government returned until the reign of Henry VII. The fire at Westminster put paid to its use as a royal residence in 1512 and it lost its role as the seat of government as Henry VIII dwelt elsewhere, mainly at Whitehall. Nonetheless Westminster retained its importance as the seat of the exchequer, the law courts and Parliament, which was to lead to the recovery of its place in the government of Britain in the seventeenth century.

The definitions of 'medieval' and 'post-medieval' are modern terms designed to make the categorisation of time easier by allotting them to convenient periods. This can be seen in the wide variety of dates given to the end of the 'medieval' period – for instance the round 1500 or the more historically important 1485 (the beginning of the Tudor dynasty after the defeat of Richard III by Henry VII at the battle of Bosworth Field). On the whole no fundamental change would have been made to the daily lives of Londoners of the time and neither 1485 nor 1500 may have been that significant to most people. However, one fundamental and hugely important change occurred in the 1530s, although no single date could be put forward: the Reformation and, with it, the Dissolution of the Monasteries. The dissolution makes a clear mark in the archaeological record and brings about an obvious change in the use of much of London as well as demonstrating archaeologically an important event in the lives of all Londoners.

English religion changed at the Reformation, but this was the product of more than a whim of Henry VIII and his advisers. Long-term jealousy at ecclesiastical power and wealth along with perceived injustices and iniquities produced a widespread backlash against the established Church, not just in England. The fall in wealth of London's religious houses was soon overturned after the disasters of the Black Death and the secularisation of their precincts and the offering of many of the administrative roles to layfolk greatly increased their prosperity. Some spent lavish sums on their religious buildings but more and more of their income seems to have been spent during the latter years of their existence on creating more wealth through leasing out their lands for domestic and industrial uses. Many of the domestic owners had only limited means but clearly Bermondsey Priory and St John's were able to lease out properties to extremely wealthy individuals within their precincts.

The value of these monastic houses was assessed at the dissolution and varied widely. Generally speaking, monastic houses valued at under £500 were closed in 1535, while those over that figure were closed between 1538 and 1540. However, the fate of the monastic houses was not always the same. Holy Trinity Priory was one of the earliest houses in England to be dissolved, in 1532. It was then granted in 1534 to Thomas Audley, who had pulled down the church, steeple and other buildings by the time of his death in 1544 (Schofield in prep). St Mary Clerkenwell was the twelfth richest English nunnery, valued at £282, but in comparison to London's other religious houses this was a fairly small sum. Its church, like that of St Helen's, was a parish church and thus escaped demolition, being handed over to its parishioners. St Mary's did not, however, escape demolition as it was pulled down and replaced by St James's in the eighteenth century. St Bartholomew the Great similarly survived although only at the eastern end, as the nave was demolished and the crossing blocked in (Fig. 59). Bermondsey Priory survived until 1538 and the final wave of closures; it was surrendered to the Crown on 1 January 1539 and was worth a similar amount to St Mary Spital, which was closed at the same time. Both had their churches demolished, and all religious ceremonies ceased on the site at that point. St John's was also dissolved and part of the church was blown up, but part of it survived and still remains the church of the Order of St John today. Westminster Abbey, of course, was not demolished at the dissolution, although it was dissolved, and at over £4,000 in value, it was the second richest in England after Glastonbury Abbey. Destruction of the royal coronation and burial church would have been unthinkable, particularly as Henry's father had built the magnificent new Lady Chapel as his dynasty's burial chapel. Westminster was therefore created a diocese with its own cathedral. Mary re-established it as a monastery in the 1550s before Elizabeth had it turned into a 'Royal Peculiar' with a dean and canons to run it.

Most of the monks, canons and friars went quietly, but at the rather more austere Charterhouse the Carthusian monks took their vows rather more seriously. They refused to sign the Oath of Supremacy and the prior and five others were burned at the stake. Prior John Houghton's arm was hacked off and nailed to the door of the priory as a grisly warning to the others if they chose to follow his path.

Fig. 59. St Bartholomew the Great after the dissolution, showing the newly built crossing wall and an open space where the demolished nave had been (photo: author)

In archaeological terms the effects of the dissolution on monastic sites are profound although not always total. The churches and main religious buildings of the monastic houses were usually immediately put out of use with the emphasis on preventing monastic communities from being able to continue to worship. Henry VIII's decision not to demolish Westminster Abbey allowed Mary to refound it. Had other churches survived destruction, many more monastic houses would, no doubt, have been refounded. The destruction often took the form of the partial or total demolition of the church and chapels and the removal of all religious effects. Often some of the church walls were retained as garden boundaries, as at St Mary Spital (Thomas *et al* 1997), or the church was effectively turned inside out with tenements built around a central space which had formerly been the church, as at Holy Trinity (Schofield in prep). Demolished, collapsed or robbed-out walls provide a vivid demonstration of the destruction of the times, and smashed statues and glass windows illustrate the iconoclasm that went with it.

Many monastic houses, as discussed earlier, had secular streets lined with houses, as at St John Clerkenwell, and these were not necessarily destroyed at the dissolution. The authorities of the time sold or gave the former monastic houses and their lands to nobles, with the result that many fine houses appeared on those sites: the Dukes of Norfolk at Charterhouse, the Dukes of Newcastle at St Mary Clerkenwell, Sir Thomas Pope at Bermondsey Priory and Stephen Vaughan at St Mary Spital.

An illustration of the effect upon the people of London might perhaps be seen in the fate of the hospitals. In 1538 the Lord Mayor, Sir Richard Gresham, petitioned Thomas Cromwell to hand over to the city the hospitals of St Mary Spital, St Bartholomew and St Thomas along with the Abbey of St Mary Graces because of the enormous relief they brought to London's poor and sick. This plea went unheeded and the effect upon Londoners must have been enormous until St Thomas's and St Bartholomew's were reopened some years later and extended to cater for the large numbers who now went uncared for.

Conclusions

At the Norman Conquest London was undoubtedly an important town. William the Conqueror considered it vital to his securing of the country and went to great lengths to capture it. He also saw Edward the Confessor's palace and coronation church at Westminster as important symbolic places. However, can we really say that London was the overwhelming metropolis and hub of England? The balance of evidence suggests probably not. Alan Vince has convincingly argued that London was one of a handful of important English towns in the later Saxon period and that it was the interest of the king which set it upon the road to its subsequent pre-eminence (Vince 1990). It was also, of course, the international trade and wealth generated in London that was one of the central reasons for the royal interest.

The early Norman period saw only gradual change but in the twelfth century things really started to happen. The arrival of stone buildings, reclamation of the river and the expansion of the docks, a profusion of parish churches and the siting of new religious complexes indicate that London was growing in both size and prosperity. The engine which drove this growth must have been trade, but hand in hand with this went political power. One of the most important decisions of any monarch was that of Henry II to build an exchequer at Westminster and then for the treasury to be relocated there. Winchester fell into decline; Westminster and London grew out of all proportion to other English cities.

Thirteenth-century London must have been an invigorating place in which to live. A population which doubled in a century, bustling streets and docks, a river teeming with traffic, immigrants from all over England and abroad must have made it a cosmopolitan place which no other English city could match. New corporate guilds were formed and London had its own government. People frequented the shops and markets and bought most of their produce with cash generated from their own employment. More products were available in terms of both food and goods. Other English cities of this period may have had little more than a quarter of its population; Bristol was perhaps London's nearest rival.

Interestingly, both London and Bristol had major suburban settlements across their respective rivers which became almost as wealthy as the main cities: Southwark at London and Redcliffe at Bristol. One of the main differences between the two was perhaps that Southwark was larger in the twelfth century than Redcliffe and thus became the site of important monastic houses and hospitals, whereas Redcliffe had only the Knights Templar, founded there in the twelfth century. The great period for Redcliffe was the later medieval period and particularly the time when the extraordinarily wealthy Canynges family lived and invested there. Southwark on the other hand had two important monastic foundations, a large hospital, a leper hospital and one of the greatest ecclesiastical palaces in the country. It was also notorious for its brothels – the stews – in the later medieval period.

The downside to all this prosperity was also that there was great poverty and disease was rife. Many of the lanes and alleys were extraordinarily cramped and accommodation was no doubt similarly confined. Sanitation was often poor and, although improving, diet for many was also not of a very high standard. Perhaps an indication of this is in people's stature. Average height for males was perhaps 1.67m, somewhat less than today: an indication that today diet and environment allow people to fulfil their potential stature far more often than in the past. At least in its charitable foundations, the hospitals, some of London's wealthier inhabitants exhibited their sense of civic and religious duty in looking after the poor. These establishments were vital for those afflicted by infirmity or extreme poverty, and were a sign of the maturity of some of its wealthier citizens.

Of course, there were also the few who were able to live in a much greater degree of comfort. Palatial residences were built along the road to Westminster, dwelt in by high-ranking nobles and bishops. They had gatehouses to enter courtyards surrounded by ranges of buildings for their own private use, for the use of their retinue and for the public. The fashions, standards and layouts were set by the monarch's palace at Westminster and no doubt there was much effort put in to outdo one's neighbour's residence. The formation of Parliament and governmental institutions was a fundamental starting point towards the centralised state and democracy.

London's monastic houses were some of the wealthiest in the country. Westminster Abbey was clearly far ahead of most other monasteries in England and enjoyed royal support in a way that no other English monastery could boast. It is, however, in the range of monastic foundations that London was so well endowed. We are also fortunate that such a large number have been investigated in such great detail that we know more about London's monastic houses in general than those of any other city, and perhaps more about them than we know of any other aspect of London's medieval archaeology. They confirm the documentary evidence that there was increasing reliance upon the market as a source of food in the later medieval period, whereas there was probably more of a reliance upon their own supplies in the twelfth and perhaps thirteenth centuries. They were highly diverse in type, and there were a large number of friaries which befitted such a large urban centre. The urban setting and occasionally the late date of some of these foundations shows how much variety there might be within a monastic order and how they might influence one another: for instance the peculiar arrangement of the Cistercian Abbey of St Mary Graces, influenced by the thirteenth-century friaries, or the urban Charterhouse with no 'courerie' or local farm so characteristic of the rural houses.

The events of 1348–9 were obviously catastrophic; no other event in London's history has been so disastrous. It is hard to imagine the fear of its citizens at the time and yet the power of the Church and its beliefs led to the victims of the Black Death being buried with the same care and religious observance shown to the dead at any other time.

The recovery of London's economy in such a short space of time after the Black Death is a testament to the power of its trading links throughout England and Europe. Late medieval London was a considerably less populous place, at least until the sixteenth century, but its increased wealth meant a better standard of living. More houses had glass windows, more were built from stone with more elaborate furnishings, and the range of utensils and other artefacts was much greater. Further reclamation and more stable and secure river frontages indicate the continued expansion in trade.

In common with other English towns, London became a more secular place. Its monasteries took on the look of small towns with precincts full of houses, workshops and traders. The Church was still the most powerful influence on most people's lives but the rumblings of discontent and the agitation for change were the beginning of the downfall of the established Church even if most of the agitants were ruthlessly dealt with initially.

The Reformation signalled an important change in religious observance and attitude as well as demonstrating the power of the English monarchs and their State. The growth of England and London from the end of the medieval period was even more meteoric under the Tudors and Stuarts but the stage had been set through the previous four hundred years.

When the Department of Urban Archaeology was formed in 1974, estimates of the survival of medieval archaeological deposits in the city were very pessimistic, largely because of the destruction caused by nineteenth-century and modern basements. Archaeological work over the subsequent twenty-five years has shown this estimate to be much more pessimistic than was actually the case. There are still areas, unexcavated as yet, where the medieval archaeology of the city survives and can tell us so much about that important period of London's past.

Outside the city, excavations have shown us that medieval London's suburbs and monastic houses survive well, sometimes to a remarkable degree. Additionally, in the other focus in the region, Westminster, archaeological deposits survive extraordinarily well in some areas allowing that settlement, the abbey and the palace to be much more fully understood.

Medieval archaeology is a relatively recent area of study. Archaeologists in the past concentrated on the prehistoric and Roman periods, perhaps believing that the standing buildings and greater documentary evidence made excavation of more recent archaeological sites unnecessary. But there are so many things that archaeology can tell us that standing structures and documents cannot, and the success of the investigation of medieval London bears testament to this. The huge increase in our knowledge and understanding of medieval London over the past twenty-five years should warn us, however, against believing that we are even close to completing the picture. As archaeologists we must always be aware that our understanding and knowledge changes with every new site that is dug and with every site from the past that we reinterpret. It would be foolhardy in the extreme to assume that we know all that there is to know about London's medieval archaeology and history, but is it possible for us to predict where there might be new avenues of research and where our understanding is weakest?

A few areas of research and ideas that might change are given here. Such a list could run to pages but here are five suggestions:

First, dating evidence is not always as secure as we might wish. Dendro-chronological and coin dates are the most secure, but we see much residuality within our finds groups and pottery specialists are constantly pushing back the earliest dates for the manufacture of certain ceramic fabrics and forms. So, for instance, our current view of a major change in twelfth-century London may yet prove to be too late.

Secondly, later medieval sites in the city are less well represented because of the effects of later development. A clearer understanding of the extent of the greater wealth and social status of many of London's inhabitants would be a major advance. This would require less truncated sites in the walled city.

Thirdly, our understanding of London's monastic houses is perhaps unrivalled in the rest of urban England. We still need to learn much more about the development of friaries which were such an important part of monasticism in urban thirteenth-century England. Also a clearer understanding of the origins and development of parish churches would not only tell us about religious provision but also about the origins of parishes and local communities. A major advance in our understanding may arise from the study of the enormous skeletal populations from these houses; one way of understanding the living is to examine the dead and our knowledge of the charitable hospitals is still very much at an early stage. What did London's leper houses look like? Did they look after lepers throughout the medieval period? How did they care for them?

Fourthly, we do not have a clear picture of the extent or style of suburban development around the city, its origins and whether expansion ceases in the later medieval period although that remains the current hypothesis. And the archaeological evidence for those farms and manors which provided the food and fuel for London's rapacious appetite is still small.

Fifthly and lastly, our knowledge of the grand mansions of London and England's ruling elite is limited to a few sites with only partial excavation. We know so little about those grand noble and ecclesiastical mansions along the Strand and Fleet Street and there is so much more to learn about the development of the royal Palace of Westminster and the rise in government. How were these buildings furnished? Can we recognise a distinct difference in the artefactual and environmental assemblages between those sites and average urban houses?

Archaeological excavation in London is rescue based – that is, it is carried out in advance of redevelopment which will destroy some or all of London's archaeological heritage. So we are governed in the first instance by development and not by archaeological questions. That is not to say, however, that we will not have the opportunity to answer some of the questions posed here either by excavation or by reanalysis. At some point in the future it is highly likely that many of our conclusions and theories will be adjusted or even rewritten by something relatively mundane or perhaps even by some remarkable new discovery.

Bibliography

Anderson, T. and Parfitt, K., 1998, 'Two unusual burials from medieval Dover', *International Journal of Osteoarchaeology* 8, 123–4

Ayre, J. and Wroe-Brown, R. with Malt, D., in prep, *Queenhithe: excavation at Thames Court, city of London, EC4, 1984–1995*

Barber, B. and Thomas, C., in prep, *Excavations at the London Charterhouse*

Barrett, M. and Thomas, C., 1991, 'The London Charterhouse', *London Archaeologist* 6, 283–91

Bateman, N., 2000, *Gladiators at the Guildhall*, London

Black, G., 1976, 'Excavations in the sub-vault of the misericorde of Westminster Abbey, February to May, 1975', *Transactions of the London and Middlesex Archaeology Society* 27, 135–78

Blatherwick, S. and Bluer, R., in prep, *Medieval Mansions of Southwark: The Rosary, Rotherhithe and Fastolf Place*

Brooke, C. and Keir, G., 1975, *London 800–1216: the shaping of a city*, London

Colvin, H.M., Allen-Brown, R. and Taylor, A.J., 1963, *The history of the King's Works*, I, London

Cowie, R. and Pipe, A., 1999, 'A late medieval and Tudor horse burial ground: excavations at Elverton Street, Westminster', *Archaeological Journal* 155, 226–51

Egan, G., 1998, *The Medieval Household: medieval finds from excavations in London*, London

Galloway, J. and Murphy, M., 1991, 'Feeding the city: medieval London and its agrarian hinterland', *London Journal* 16, 3–14

Goffin, R.A., 1991, 'A group of pottery from a medieval pit at 223–227 Borough High Street, Southwark', *London Archaeologist* 6, 315–18

Goffin, R.A., 1995, 'The accessioned finds', in P. Mills, 'Excavations at the dorter undercroft, Westminster Abbey', *Transactions of the London and Middlesex Archaeological Society* 46, 87–90

Goodburn, D. with Thomas, C., 1997, 'Reused medieval ship planks from Westminster, England, possibly derived from a vessel built in the cog style', *International Journal of Nautical Archaeology* 26 (1), 26–38

Grainger, I., Hawkins, D. and Mills, P., in prep, *The Abbey of St Mary Graces*

Green, H.J.M., 1976, 'Excavations of the palace defences and abbey precinct walls at Abingdon St, Westminster, 1963', *Journal of the British Archaeological Association* 129, 59–76

Grimes, W.F., 1968, *The Excavation of Roman and Medieval London*, London

Hawkins, D., 1990, 'The Black Death and the new London cemeteries of 1348', *Antiquity* 64, 637–42

Hill, J. and Woodger, A., 1999, *Excavations at 72–75 Cheapside/83–93 Queen Street, city of London*, MoLAS Archaeology Study Series 2

Horsman, V. and Davison, B., 1989, 'New Palace Yard and its fountains: excavations in the Palace of Westminster', *Antiquarian Journal* 69

Horsman, V., Milne, C. and Milne, G., 1988, *Aspects of Saxo-Norman London: 1 Building and street development*, London and Middlesex Archaeological Society special paper 11

Jones, D.M., 1980, *Excavations at Billingsgate Buildings 'triangle', Lower Thames St, 1974*, London and Middlesex Archaeological Society special paper 4

Keene, D., 1984, 'A new study of London before the Great Fire', *Urban History Yearbook 1984*

Keene, D. 1989, 'Medieval London and its region', *London Journal* 14, 99–111

Kingsford, C.L., 1971, *John Stow: a survey of London*, vol. 1 [1603]

Marsden, P., 1994, 'Ships of the Port of London: first to eleventh centuries AD', *EH Archaeology Report 3*

Marsden, P., 1996, 'Ships of the Port of London: twelfth to seventeenth centuries AD', *EH Archaeology Report 5*

Mills, P., 1995, 'Excavations at the Dorter undercroft, Westminster Abbey', *Transaction of the London and Middlesex Archaeological Society* 46, 69–124

Mills, P., 1996, 'The Battle of London 1066', *London Archaeologist* 8, 59–62

Milne, G. and Milne, C., 1981, *Medieval waterfront development at Trig Lane, London*, London and Middlesex Archaeological Society special paper 5

MoLAS, 2000, *The archaeology of Greater London: an assessment of archaeological evidence for human presence in the area now covered by Greater London*, MoLAS Monograph

Norman, P.J., 1916, 'Recent discoveries of medieval remains in London', *Archaeologia*, 67, 14–17

Palliser, D.M. (ed.), 2000, *The Cambridge Urban History of Britain, vol. 1 600–1540*, Cambridge University Press

Parnell, G., 1983, 'The western defences of the inmost ward, Tower of London', *Transactions of the London and Middlesex Archaeological Society* 34, 107–50

Price, J.E., 1870, 'Medieval kiln for burning encaustic tiles discovered near Farringdon Road, Clerkenwell', *Transactions of the London and Middlesex Archaeological Society* 3, 31–6

Rosser, G., 1989, *Medieval Westminster*, London

Rowsome, P., 2000, *Heart of the City: Roman, medieval and modern London revealed by archaeology at 1 Poultry*, London

Samuel, M., 1989, 'The fifteenth-century garner at Leadenhall, London', *Antiquaries Journal* 69 (1), 119–53

Schofield, J., 1984, *The building of London from the Conquest to the Great Fire*, London

Schofield, J., Allen, P. and Taylor, C., 1990, 'Medieval buildings and property development in the area of Cheapside', *Transactions of the London and Middlesex Archaeological Society* 41, 39–237

Schofield, J. and Vince, A. in Schofield 1990, finds dating and environmental evidence catalogue

Schofield, J., in prep, *Excavations at Holy Trinity Priory, Aldgate*

Seeley, D., in prep, *Excavations at Winchester Palace Southwark*

Sloane, B., in prep, *Excavations at the nunnery of St Mary de fonte clericorum, Clerkenwell*

Sloane, B. and Malcolm, G., in prep, *Excavation at the Priory of the Order of the Hospital of St John of Jerusalem, Clerkenwell*

Steedman, K., Dyson, T. and Schofield J., 1992, *Aspects of Saxo-Norman London: III The Bridgehead and Billingsgate to 1200*, London and Middlesex Archaeological Society special paper 14

Steele, A., in prep, *Excavations at Bermondsey Abbey*

Stukeley, W.M., 1790, 'The sanctuary at Westminster', *Archaeologia* 1, 43–8

Tanner, L.E. and Clapham, A.W., 1935, 'Recent discoveries in the Nave of Westminster Abbey', *Archaeologia* 83, 227–36

Tatton-Brown, T., 1995, 'Westminster Abbey: archaeological recording at the west end of the church', *Antiquaries Journal* 75, 171–88

Thomas, A.H., 1923, 'Notes on the history of the Leaden-hall 1195–1488', *London Topographical Record* 13, 1–23

Thomas, C., Sloane, B. and Phillpotts, C., 1997, *Excavations at the Priory and Hospital of St Mary Spital, London*, MoLAS Monograph 1

Thomas, C. and Holder, N., 1999, 'Spitalfields', *Current Archaeology* 162, 211–14

Thomas, C., Cowie, R. and Sidell, J., in prep, *The Royal Palace, Abbey and Town of Westminster on Thorney Island: archaeological investigations (1991–1998) in advance of the London Underground Limited Jubilee Line Extension*

Thurley, S., 1999, *Whitehall Palace, An Architectural History of the Royal Apartments, 1240–1690*, Yale University Press

Vince, A., 1990, *Saxon London: an archaeological investigation*

Vulliamy, G., 1849, 'Proceedings of the Archaeological Institute', *Archaeological Journal* 6, 71

Watson, B., 1994, 'Excavations and observations on the site of the Dutch church, Austin Friars, in the city of London', *Transactions of the London and Middlesex Archaeological Society* 45, 13–22

Watson, B., Brigham, T. and Dyson, T., 2001, *London Bridge: 2000 years of a river crossing*, MoLAS Monograph 8

White, W., 1988, *The cemetery of St Nicholas Shambles*, London and Middlesex Archaeological Society special paper 9

Wilson, C., 1996, *The Gothic Cathedral*, London

Index

Numbers in italics denote figures